Everything You Want Is Really Jewish

Everything You Want Is Really Jewish

Tzvi Gluckin

Copyright © 2009 by Tzvi Gluckin
First Edition, April 2009
Second Edition, Novemenber 2011

ISBN-13: 978-0-9845856-3-2

All rights reserved. No part of the material protected by this copyright notice may be reproduced or utilized in any form, electronic or mechanical, including photocopying, recording, or by any information storage and retrieval system, without written permission from the copyright owner.

Mekabel Press
100 Hano Street, Suite 28
Allston, MA 02134

You can contact the author at tzvi.gluckin@gmail.com

Typesetting and book design by Larissa Zaretsky
Cover Design by Shira Greenberg www.shiragreenberg.com

An earlier version of *Shwarma: A Love Story* appears on the website aish.com and is featured in the book *Heaven on Earth* (published by Targum Press). It is reprinted here with permission from the editors.

Printed in the United States of America
15 14 13 12 11   10 9 8 7 6 5 4 3 2

This book is dedicated to the
memory of my father-in-law,
Mr. Ian Hyams.

Table of Contents

Intro	1
Part One	7
Part Two	71
Outro	83
Appendix	87
Shwarma: A Love Story	89
Groovy Photos	93
Endnotes	99
Acknowledgements	105
About the Author	111
Rabbinical Endorsements	113
Dedications	117

Intro

I am old enough to remember World War II veterans. They were my grandparents, great aunts and uncles, and their friends. They grew up during the Depression and fought in World War II. In the 1970's – when I was a kid – they were in their fifties, still healthy, still working, crazy, and enjoying their grandchildren. They were different from the generation that came after them. They didn't understand the hippies or the social upheavals of the 1960's. They were not radical. They worked hard. They knew what it meant to be poor. They were patriotic and they took their patriotism for granted.

And they were Jewish. They lived in Jewish neighborhoods in and around New York, in exotic places like Canarsie, East New York, and Jersey City. Their friends were Jewish. Their parents were Jewish immigrants from Russia and Poland. And they knew some Yiddish.

They also had a strong Jewish identity. Although they didn't know much about Judaism, they fasted on Yom Kippur, ate matzo on Passover, and some of them had two sets of dishes. They were proud. Judaism was a staple you took for granted. It was like being patriotic. You did it. You didn't ask questions. They had a strong bond to their tradition, their parents, their roots, and Jewish food. The bond was emotional, but it was strong and it meant something to them. They would never marry a non-Jew; they didn't understand how anyone could.

As you would expect, they raised their children to be Jewish. They took them to synagogue on the High Holidays, sent them to Hebrew School (at least the boys), fed them matzo balls, and worried about them. Their children had a similar emotional connection to Judaism – though not as strong and they didn't speak Yiddish – and usually only married Jewish as well. These children were better educated, made more money, and moved to the suburbs.

But the suburbs might as well have been Mars. The grandchildren of the World War II veterans – i.e. me – grew up in an alien universe.

I grew up as an American. The town I lived in didn't have a Jewish neighborhood. My school was open on the Jewish holidays. My friends didn't have names like Goldstein and Greenberg; they had names like Fitzgerald, Vezzuto, Smith, and Van Doren. I was a normal American kid. I watched movies, took guitar lessons, begged my parents to get MTV, worried about acne, took the SATs, spent my money on concerts, and drove around on weekends looking for parties. I fit in. Or so I thought. I didn't understand why my parents made me go to Hebrew school, miss school for the Jewish holidays, begged me not to intermarry, or forced me to have a Bar Mitzvah. I didn't get it. These things were odd, branded me as different, and were a waste of time.

The Jewish identity my grandparents took for granted didn't make it to me. It got lost in suburban New Jersey.

The mixed signals I got from my parents, school, friends, and TV were confusing. Who was I? What did I believe in? I was happy. I was normal. I knew my parents loved me. But I didn't know who I was.

This book is about what I did to find out. As you will see, I got more than I bargained for.

Part One

I am from New Jersey. I have New Jersey pride. I was embarrassed when New Jersey countered New York's successful "I Love NY" campaign with the lame "I am a New Jersey Tomato."

I grew up in the suburbs. I listened to heavy metal and I didn't like Bruce Springsteen (the jingle bells on *Born To Run* drove me crazy). I thought I was a rebel – albeit a lame rebel – I didn't smoke, take drugs, or read Marxist literature. And I wanted long hair. I wanted long hair because long hair was cool (and not because I loved the sixties, I didn't, and Joan Baez really ticked me off with her "Woodstock" comment at Live Aid).

My parents said a nice Jewish boy should have short hair. Not cool. We compromised and it was the worst of both worlds. My hair was thick and curly – Jewish hair – my parents let me grow it until it covered the top of my ears and to the collar in the back, but never longer. I looked horrible: it either had to be short and neat or long to look good. Not halfway. It was a mess of half curls and things poking out at weird angles. I was stubborn and kept up the battle throughout high school. As a result, I spent four years looking like a buffoon.

I was a weird kid. I never went outside, I hated sports, the jocks in high school made fun of me (and my hair was ridiculous). I loved music, though no one knew until junior high. At thirteen, I decided I had to play the guitar. I told my parents I was going to buy one and my father gave me a job working for him. He paid me a dollar an hour and I worked in a chemical factory sweeping floors and cleaning out a giant mixing machine that processed spirulina. (Spirulina is thick, pasty, green algae coveted by health nuts. After a day's work I was green from head to toe, as were my sinuses, clothes, and anything I came into contact with). I also mowed lawns in the neighborhood and did odd jobs to earn money. I worked the entire summer and earned about $400. I bought my first guitar, amp, and started taking lessons.

I took guitar playing seriously. I practiced about four hours a day and was in a band with my friends. I wrote music and learned how to improvise. I also learned the tuba, contrabass clarinet, and baritone sax. I was in my high school marching band, jazz band, and the New Jersey All-State wind ensemble.

My parents encouraged my music and guitar playing until I told them I was going to music school and that music would be my profession. They thought I should go to a normal college and get a useful degree. We battled for months but in the end reached a compromise (and it was a better compromise than the one about my hair): I could apply to one music school in addition to the other colleges I would apply to. If I could get in, great, if not, I would go to a real college and get on with my life.

I chose the best music school I could find (the New England Conservatory of Music in Boston), applied, and auditioned.

My audition was horrible. I was terrified and could barely get a note out. I stumbled over my prepared chorus of *Donna Lee* (Charlie Parker's Be Bop classic made famous by Jaco Pastorius). I fumbled and lost the groove. (In my dreams I thought I would blow them away with my honed Jaco chops. Unlike Jaco I lacked the confidence or skill to pull it off.) Even worse, for my second piece I noodled aimlessly over the Miles Davis modal classic *So What*. I was embarrassed. I played so poorly that I didn't bother taking the tour of the school they offered after the auditions; I was convinced I was not going to get accepted. I went back to New Jersey dejected.

But I was mistaken. I got in.

I was lucky. I got accepted because the regular guitar faculty wasn't at my audition. They were mean and tough and had no tolerance for sloppy guitar playing and even less for almost-longhaired wannabes from New Jersey. They would not have accepted me.

Jim and Jimmy – from the jazz department but not the guitar staff – ran my audition. They let me in. Jim got stoned for the auditions. He didn't remember being there so everyone he auditioned got in. Jimmy was the nicest man in the world: he was sunshine and good vibes and accepted everyone he auditioned too.

I was thrilled. My parents kept their half of the deal and I moved to Boston. I grew my hair – it was the first thing I did in college. I was liberated. It was great.

Three months into my freshman year I asked a guy who lived in my dorm to trim the back and the bangs. The haircut was a disaster. I looked like a woman (an ugly woman). Why did I let an incompetent boob touch my hair? He was a musician not a barber. I wanted to kill him. I wanted to kill everyone like him. But there was nothing to do, I vowed to go a year without a haircut and I did.

At the end of the year my hair was a wild, beastly mess. I grew a mustache. I was beautiful. In my junior year I got fed up with my hair and shaved the sides. I shaved them bald but kept the top and back long. Nowadays, my haircut is called a "mullet," but I take offense. In the late eighties a "mullet" was simply the haircut-the-cool-guys-have. My hair – which I appropriately dubbed a long wide Mohawk – was a source of pride and a symbol of my individuality.

I was a Jazz Studies major and I worked hard. I looked for gigs and joined a few bands – mostly blues-based electric funk wannabe pioneer types – in addition to Fat Elvis, a goofy punk band. Aside from Fat Elvis, my playing was insincere and inauthentic – especially in traditional jazz settings. At least that's what they told me.

"You play too white." I do? What was it about the genre that I hadn't internalized? It bugged me. Maybe it was because I didn't know enough about being black. I learned about Mingus, Dolphy, Monk, and Coltrane. I read radical writers like Leroy Jones and Mingus's *Beneath the Underdog*. It wasn't enough. I listened to Public Enemy and made my parents watch Spike Lee movies. For whatever reason, I didn't have soul. A resurgence of sixties radicalism was in the air and jazz musicians in the press were openly critical of white people trying to play jazz. This attitude was at the Conservatory too. If you weren't black you were forever trying to play *more black* – and you could never be black enough. I was introduced to James Brown, P Funk, and innovators like Cecil Taylor and Albert Ayler. I practiced six hours a day, listened to music constantly, and did my best to absorb black culture (short of visiting the soul food joints in Roxbury). I became more proficient and achieved a level of mastery on my instrument, but culturally the black thing drove me crazy. "You play pretty good, for a white guy." I was jealous. Who was I trying to be anyway?

I met Al in college. Al was a longhaired alienated white kid from Long Island (and he had a mean leather jacket). He transferred to the Conservatory from Berklee to study microtonal composition. We first met at a party in a luxury condo across the street from Fenway Park. The condo was a massive loft and our host was an eccentric percussionist, the son of a Japanese millionaire. The people at the party were Cambridge intellectuals; most of them were rich, gay, and crazy. I was wearing a Metallica t-shirt. No one talked to me until I bumped into Al. "You like Metallica?" "I love Metallica. I saw them open for Ozzy last year." "Why are you here?" "I have no idea. Everyone here is crazy." This went on for about an hour and by the end of the night we were best friends. From then on we hung out and bonded over Schoenberg, music theory, microtones, Hendrix, custom guitars, and gourmet beer.

Al was Italian. He was close with his family and didn't question his identity (Al didn't want to be black). I was jealous. I wanted to be like Al. Al didn't listen to P Funk or pretend to be a late sixties hipster, he was who he was. But me? I didn't have an identity. I was a Jewish kid from New Jersey. What did that mean?

(After college, when we were both living in New York, Al often took me to his parents' house on Long Island. His grandfather lived with them and spoke Italian. They loved to feed me. When I came to visit we ate five course meals of fish, pasta, cheese, bread, crazy things I can't pronounce, espresso, and cake. After eating we sat on the couch, unable to move, and in pain. "I can't move. I can't keep my eyes open." They thought that being Jewish was the funniest thing in the world. Al's father called me "Jerusalem." I called him a wop. He thought that was great.)

In my senior year I got to spend three weeks with Taylor McKnight. We rehearsed for eight hours a day. Every day Taylor brought photocopies of lines and shapes and arrows moving in crazy directions and we had to play it. He conducted as our ensemble wadded through a cacophony of noise and space. It didn't matter. Every day Taylor had new photocopies; the shapes were new and the arrows pointed in different directions.

I played the same thing every day. I made noise. I used a slide above the register where the frets end. I goofed around with feedback, wide intervals, and exotic wah-wah sounds. Taylor thought I was a genius. "Where's my number?" he asked. I loved him but realized I would never work for him because I didn't dig his lifestyle. He took too much cocaine and stayed up all night drinking eighty-dollar bottles of Champagne – not for me.

Taylor was cool because he was old, black, and a legend in the jazz world. He had white people in his band even back in the sixties and he thought that racism in music was stupid. I agreed with Taylor – how convenient – but it didn't help. My inferiority complex wasn't because I wasn't black; it was because I didn't know who I was.

I was ready to move on. Boston was no place for a hot shot twenty-two year old. Boston is a boring college town. The subway closes at midnight and the neighborhoods are quiet and peaceful. I had to move to New York. It sucked me in. I was seduced, allured, mesmerized, and fascinated with New York. I dreamed about New York. I talked about New York. I was obsessed with New York.

I graduated in May 1990 and moved to Brooklyn. I got a job teaching guitar lessons and taught about thirty students a week. Most of my students were Cuban kids who wanted to play salsa music and young budding metal heads. I loved my students and spent hours talking with them about their lives and dreams. Many of my students – especially the older ones – only continued with lessons so they could talk with me. They weren't interested in guitar and never practiced. I guess people are lonely. Confiding in your guitar teacher is better than going to a shrink.

To make ends meet I sold tickets for the New York Philharmonic. I was in charge of the group sales department, which meant I called lists of tri-state area band directors and convinced them to bring their students to see the orchestra. I got fat commissions and free tickets to everything at Lincoln Center.

The rest of the time I played in bands around New York and New Jersey. I was part of a clique of ten guys who moved from Boston to New York that summer and we played together constantly. We had four piece rock bands, weird experimental improvisation units, funk groups, and a blues trio. The rest of the time Botz (my roommate and drummer) and I recorded on an eight-track machine we had in our rehearsal space. We recorded everything from country western tunes, to Captain Beefheart inspired ditties, to pop metal, to reworked old blues songs, to you name it. Although the music was diverse, the lyrics were usually odes to our anatomy.

I met Botz when I was looking for an apartment. Another friend from college and I decided to room together and we needed a third person to afford the rent. Botz was a drummer and had recently moved to New York after finishing his degree at Berklee. He stayed in Boston an extra year to try to make it with his band and his wife moved to the Midwest to go to law school. Within a few months she left him. I met Botz the week the divorce papers came through. I am sure he was miserable, but you would never know it.

Botz was the quintessential glass-half-full kind of guy. He was loud, brash, opinionated, positive, and knew something about everything. He could cook, fix a car, knew the best way to wash dishes, loved White Castle, and came up with new uses for coffee filters (he used them as toilet paper). He invented new expressions: toilet paper had a special name, cigarettes were cylindrical tubes of coolness, the list went on. Botz was six foot five and weighed well over 200 pounds. He was an amazing drummer.

Botz was five years older than me and saw Zeppelin on their last tour in 1977. He had tickets to see them again on their aborted final tour when Bonham died. It was his claim to fame. He wasn't impressed that I saw Ozzy or Iron Maiden, he saw Zeppelin at Madison Square Garden in 1977. I ate my heart out.

I was immediately drawn to Botz. We were kindred spirits on a quest for the essence of life and we both intuitively understood that the secret was to be found in loud, edgy, blues-based music.

Botz drove a banana-yellow 1978 Dodge Aspen wagon. He bought it for $500 and had a day job selling life insurance. He was too nice a guy and couldn't close a sale, so he starved and never paid rent until I got him a job with me at the Philharmonic.

Botz's mission was to teach me how to drive like a New Yorker. "You tailgate cabs until you are good enough to cut them off." He told me this as we were flying across the Manhattan Bridge about to hit the sharp right just as the bridge comes into the city. "You'll never get a traffic ticket in New York. The cops are too busy dealing with real crime. Always make sure you are the first at a red light. If all the lanes are full, make your own lane. If you can't make your own lane, edge onto the sidewalk. The kiss of death is getting stuck behind someone when the light turns green, you can sit there forever." He went on and on like this. "Watch the signs. When 'Don't Walk' starts flashing in the other direction, start rolling. You will be ready to gun it as soon as you get the green. If you are good you can count the seconds from when 'Don't Walk' goes solid and your light goes green." He also watched the 'Don't Walk' signs when we were cruising up the avenues. As soon as they started flashing he went even faster so as to make a few extra blocks before the dreaded red.

I followed Botz's advice and became the most aggressive driver alive. First I cut off cabs and then I cut off cops. Botz was right. The cops didn't care.

Botz was the only drummer I worked with for three years. We played music constantly. When we weren't playing music we were talking about it and usually arguing. Botz had a soft spot for the dinosaur progressive rock bands from the seventies. I was too young and didn't get it. I tried to turn him on to early-eighties hardcore and the new punk-funk scene that was emerging at that time, but it wasn't for him. To him, his saddest day was when his ex-wife sold his collection of original Zappa on vinyl.

We lived in a three-bedroom apartment in Park Slope. The gentrification of Park Slope had already started but hadn't yet made its way to 16th Street where we lived. Our block was still crazy New Yorkers and drug dealers. The guy across the street had a van he was slowly converting into a tank. We were convinced he was a genius, especially once we learned his mastery of the alternate side of the street parking laws. He never got a ticket.

We wrote on the walls of our apartment: usually silly pictures, phone numbers, and poems about the subway. We were cool.

Al moved to New York at this time. He lived with his parents on Long Island. We were both new to the city and wandered the back alleys of the cool parts of town a few nights week. We thought we were Columbus. We veered out from the safety of Greenwich Village and moved east down East 8th Street. We discovered the East Village, Alphabet City, and Tompkins Square Park. We found hip vegetarian joints, cheap bars, jazz haunts, and super pretentious poet's cafes (Botz often hung with us in the cool parts of town, but he had no tolerance for the chi-chi coffee joints. "How can you pay five dollars for a cup of cauffee?") Our greatest discovery was a small bar in the trendy part of the Village. It had a drinking age of twenty-five and only served Belgian imports in Champagne bottles and fancy German beer on tap. I became a beer snob and learned the essentials of sophisticated living.

After a year Botz and I needed to find a new roommate. The other guy – the one who initially got us together – moved out and we needed to fill his room. He was our bass player and he stayed in the band for another year or so, but he needed his own space – I don't blame him, we were crazy. We took out an ad in the *Village Voice* and that is how we found B.

B was nothing like us. She wasn't a suburban white kid with a fancy music degree. She was young, black, smart, and in with every radical thinker and movement in New York. B wrote wild emotional feminist poetry. She entered poetry slams and was usually a finalist. She was angry and radical but also really normal. Her parents were a cute interracial couple from upstate. They helped her move in. They were happy that Botz and I were music nerds and not drugged out hipsters.

B's friends met in our living room to discuss politics, women's issues, civil rights, black power, public nudity, legalizing pot, and every other hip cause written about in the *Voice*. They smoked, wore cool clothes, wrote poetry, and were angry. I was in heaven. Botz and I were the token white guys. They thought we were cute and tolerated us. We never participated in their debates (not that we were asked to join).

As time went on, B's friends got more daring. They wanted to take over City College. They were very serious. They planned for weeks. I don't know if they ever did it but they liked that we wrote on the walls and started writing slogans of their own.

"Black is for Africa. White is for the Devil."

This was on the wall one day. I was jealous. B and her black friends were on to something. They knew who they were and they were proud of it. They fought for it. They could articulate it. They had opinions, ideas, and an identity.

I did not know who I was. I had no idea. I knew I was a Jewish kid from New Jersey. But that was about it. What does that mean? I never considered myself much of anything. In the context of the times – and because of B's influence – I decided that I wasn't white. I was an oppressed minority struggling to get out from under the thumb of the MAN. I was a Jew. I wanted to assert my ethnicity too.

"I laugh at your four hundred years of suffering. My people suffered for three thousand years."

I never had the guts to say this to B. I thought it was funny. B would have killed me. Worse, she would have made me listen to a lengthy dissertation about tolerance as penance. I am glad I kept my mouth shut.

In college I wanted to be black. But that didn't work. I wasn't an Italian like Al either. I was Jewish. That was my ethnicity. What does it mean to be ethnic? I knew about Jewish food. I went to the knish joints on Delancey Street;

they had big, fat knishes stuffed with love, kasha, potatoes, and onions. I connected.

I took Al to a Ukrainian restaurant I knew about in Manhattan. It was not a Jewish place, but they served "Jewish" sounding food like kasha and matzo ball soup. I bought Al a plate of kasha. He was disgusted. By his second mouthful most of the kasha fell out of his mouth onto the plate.

"You are feeding me sand."

"Not all food needs to be dripping in garlic to taste good." He wouldn't hear it, he was disgusted: the Jewish culinary tradition (especially as interpreted via a Ukrainian restaurant) was not in the lexicon of "good" in Al's world. We decided to talk music and beer, but food was taboo.

I thought about being Jewish. Was I a hip, oppressed, ethnic minority? I was something, right? I didn't know what to do with my feelings so I let them stagnate. Botz was Jewish too, but it didn't mean anything to him. We never talked about it.

And then I met Josh. In a few years I would freak him out with an intense blast of Jewishness, but initially we thought the same way.

Josh was into art. His parents were rich and bought him a swank one-bedroom apartment on the Upper East Side. He had a doorman and everything. In his apartment were canvases, sketches, and works in progress. Josh ate noodles, American cheese, and was convinced he was poor. He was really into being poor.

We met because Josh wanted to take guitar lessons; in a frenzy of painting he started listening to Frank Zappa, decided Zappa was the most important musician of our generation, and decided he had to start playing guitar (like Zappa). Josh had no fear. He called up Frank Zappa's record label and left long rambling messages about how he needed guitar lessons. They thought he was crazy and didn't return his calls. Josh was persistent. He called back every day and left a message. Eventually he got through. He mentioned his plight: that he was an artist, loved Zappa, and needed to learn how to play the guitar. The people at the label told him to call Mark – a keyboardist living in Boston – to get rid of him. Mark knew Botz. Josh called Mark. Mark told him that a) he didn't play guitar and b) that he lived in Boston so even if he did, the commute wouldn't be worth it for a one-hour lesson.

Mark told Josh to call me. He told him that I was in Brooklyn and would be happy to help. Which was true. Josh called me, pleaded with me, begged me, told me about Zappa and the label and how much he needed to play the guitar. I told him I would love to help. I charged him $20 an hour and stopped by his swank Manhattan apartment at night on my way home from teaching my other students.

Josh was just like me. He was Jewish. He loved art, music, and liberal politics. We were the same age. Within a few weeks he stopped paying for lessons and we just hung out. I turned him on to crazy new music, jazz, and especially the blues. He turned me on to art, cable TV, and the Upper East Side. I loved Jackson Pollack. Josh didn't. We both loved the blues. We dug Muddy Waters, Howlin' Wolf, Leadbelly, John Lee Hooker, and Screamin' Jay Hawkins.

Josh and I hung out all the time. I asked him about being Jewish. He knew less than I did and didn't want to think about it. He told me to read, that it would open my mind to new worlds. I didn't know what to read. I knew Al read all the time so I asked him. Al read Bukowski. He read every book Bukowski wrote. He told me to read Bukowski too. I did. Bukowski led to Hemmingway. Hemmingway led to Céline. Céline led to Henry Miller. I was hooked. I read all the time. I wanted to meet Bukowski.

I convinced Al that we should drive to New Orleans for Mardi Gras, get blood alcohol poisoning, recover, and then drive to California. In California we would find Bukowski. He would insult us and we would end up as two goofball East Coast losers in one of his novels. It was our dream but we never did it. It was like a lot of my plans; I had big ideas but never did much of anything.

Reading got me thinking. I thought I was a philosopher. Was there something bigger in the world? What was it? I couldn't articulate what I was thinking. Was it spiritual? Maybe. I didn't like that word – spiritual – it sounded too medieval. I decided there was no God. Religion was mythology and the cause of all the world's troubles. There was no afterlife. When you died you were dead – that's it. Logically, I concluded that there were no consequences to my actions. I could do whatever I wanted, get away with it, and not feel guilty. But I was a wimp. My guilty conscience gnawed at me. It kept me from trying anything radical or dangerous. I hated my guilty conscience. If I could learn to be apathetic, I would be liberated. I could live like a rock star.

But I couldn't do it.

I hung a sign on my wall that said, "Apathy is an Art." I didn't act on it. Botz understood. He didn't act on it either.

I kept reading and I kept thinking. I realized I hated New York. I had to escape. I was sick of playing in bands, teaching lessons, and working for the Philharmonic. I needed to move on. I needed to stop feeling guilty.

Travel. That was the answer. In all the books I read, especially Henry Miller, the answer was travel. The answers were on the road. I would hit the road and learn. I was twenty-four and it was the summer of 1992. My twenty-fifth birthday was in six months. If I felt the same way on my birthday I was going to travel.

But six months was a long time. I needed to do something now to shake things up. I decided to cut my hair. I still had the super-wide Mohawk from college. It was time to go. I was sick of it. The back was one big dreadlock.

I went to visit my parents and told my mom my plan. She was thrilled. I needed glasses too and I was procrastinating about getting them: my mother offered to pay for the glasses and the haircut. We went to the eyeglass place and I took a test. They told me to come back in an hour. I went to the barber and shaved my entire head. When I went back for the glasses they didn't recognize me.

My friends in New York didn't recognize me either. I went to the Knitting Factory where Botz was playing a reunion gig with his band from Boston. I showed up and hung out. No one knew who I was. I was anonymous amongst my friends. I talked to Botz between sets. It took him a minute to realize who I was – he was freaked out. That was the beginning.

Six months flew by in a flash and it was my twenty-fifth birthday. I took the day off from the Philharmonic and hung out in Park Slope eating Thai food. After lunch I went home and B was in a foul mood because none of the TV channels were working. It was the day Arab terrorists attacked the World Trade Center for the first time. They planted a van loaded with explosives in the parking garage, blew it up, killed a few people, and knocked out power in the building (the TV tower was on the roof – hence no TV for B).

This was a sign. It was time to get out of New York. Amsterdam was going to be my first stop. I bought an open-ended round trip ticket that was good for a year.

By May, I was on the road.

✧ 2 ✧

I quit my job at the Philharmonic, said goodbye to my students, told the musicians I worked with that I was leaving, moved out of my apartment, and got rid of my car. I was going to Europe. I was really going to do it.

My plan was to play guitar on the streets for money, at least enough to earn room and board for the night. I was going to meet new people, freeload when possible, and flop at youth hostels when necessary. I was going to use my gift of the gab, magnetic charm, and exceptional people skills to network, connect, and get my way in with Europe's underground hipsters. I would become a counter-cultural hero, following in the footsteps of Ernest Hemingway, Henry Miller, and the other great American expatriates.

I bought a Euro-rail pass and a copy of *Let's Go Europe* as a backup for those odd times when things didn't work out. I packed my guitar and a battery-powered amplifier, three pairs of underwear, two pairs of socks, two t-shirts, a pair of jeans, shorts, a toothbrush and toothpaste, and a bar of soap that doubled as shampoo. I had deodorant too. I was ready to conquer the world.

I flew into Amsterdam. I made my way through customs, got my first stamp in my brand new passport, found my way to the train, and took the short trip to the main train station in the center of town.

I left the station and walked down the main drag. All around were small hotels, coffee houses, and an endless number of places to exchange money. I stopped to call home and let everyone know I was alive and well. My first Atlantic crossing wasn't a big deal. I wandered on.

I walked until I reached a large fountain in the center of the city. Everywhere was action, people, youth, color, everything. Everyone was busy. Music, jugglers, fire-eaters, freaks, hippies, all the riff-raff that find their way to alternative centers like Amsterdam. The city was alive and excitement was in the air. Everyone spoke English. Thousands of bicycles littered the streets.

"This could be the beginning of everything," I thought. "Maybe I should take out my guitar and start playing. This could be it."

I decided to wait. It was my first day. I had just landed and was probably jet lagged.

I walked around for a while. I sat down near the big fountain. I walked around a little more. I sat down near the fountain again.

"This place is fantastic!" I said to myself. "My friends would love it here."

I looked around. People were eating French fries. (Europeans eat French fries out of large paper tubes and dip them in crazy sauces.) My stomach was rumbling. I hadn't eaten since the flight and that was a while ago. I looked for a place to buy French fries. I walked down a side street, around a corner and down another side street. Nothing.

I followed a few people I saw eating French fries. No luck. I couldn't find anything. I wandered around for about a half an hour. My mouth was watering and my stomach was grumbling.

"Maybe you should ask somebody," I thought.

I decided to look around a little more. I went up and down a few streets. I retraced my steps and looked for something or someone who could help me find French fries. I couldn't find anything.

"Everyone speaks English. Ask somebody."

It was getting hot. It was a beautiful day, not a cloud in the sky, but the midday sun was starting to take its toll on my road-weary body.

I found my way back to the fountain and sat down. I looked around. Bicycles, thousands of bicycles, everywhere I looked were cheap black three-speeders with goofy handlebars.

"Amsterdam is a wild place," I thought to myself.

More bicycles, unicyclists, mimes, musicians, and clowns were gathering around my fountain. Small clusters of American tourists congregated on benches and near buildings. I was surrounded by hair, color, laughter, smoke, and the sounds of white urban youth on holiday and away from home.

The day went on. I was starting to fade. It had been a long flight. The excitement of a new city and the promise of adventure were wearing off. I needed to lie down and get some rest. I was confident that if I looked around I could find a youth hostel for ten or fifteen dollars a night.

I got up and walked around again. My bag and guitar were getting heavy. I looked in windows and doorways for something that looked like a hostel. No luck. I wasn't sure what I was looking for.

"You're surrounded by American tourists," I thought. "Ask them where they are staying."

I walked down street after street, over bridges, and through narrow tunnels. I admired the canals and intricate citywide water system. I wandered in giant circles for an hour and somehow made my way back to my fountain. I was exhausted. The sun, lack of food, and time difference was beginning to take its toll. I just wanted a place to lie down.

"Look in your *Let's Go Europe*. This is the reason you brought it."

There is an unwritten rule when riding New York's subways: never look at the maps posted by the MTA. No self-respecting New Yorker would ever be caught dead with his nose up to the wall, pointing at stations, or talking out loud about where to get off. To do so would be justifiable grounds for public humiliation, a breach in the self-confidant, all-knowing façade required of hip urban dwellers. Intuitively, this principle is applicable to the self-styled, expatriate radical wanderer as well.

There was no way I was going to look through my *Let's Go Europe* in public.

I sat by the fountain for a while. People were coming and going. The tourists were in the museums. The tattooed, heavily pierced people in black crawled from their caves and were meeting each other by the fountain. I was starving.

"I have to lie down," I said to myself.

I picked up my stuff and headed back down the main drag towards the train station, past the money exchange places and expensive looking establishments. I walked for a few minutes until I came to a place called the Delta Hotel.

"Hmm…" I thought, "The Delta Hotel, nice. Like the Delta Blues, cool… very cool."

I went in and paid for a room. It worked out to be about $60 for the night. I went up a narrow staircase, entered my room, put down my stuff, checked out the bathroom, noticed the arched ceilings, and looked out the window.

I sat down on the bed and started to cry. I was a loser.

I cried and I cried. What was I thinking? What happened to the slick talking, suave, self-confident smoothie? I was supposed to meet people, network, and get myself in. Instead, I was alone in the Delta Hotel for $60 a night. I didn't have the guts to ask about a tube of French fries, let alone scam a free room or play guitar on the street. What was I going to do? I was thousands of miles from home – not that I had anything to go back to – I had no apartment, job, car, or anything else, I had made sure of that, and the

SHAME, if I were to go back now – the SHAME – oh my. There was no turning back. What was I going to do?

I was pathetic. I laid down on the bed sniffling and feeling sorry for myself.

What was I afraid of? Maybe a big green monster with six heads would jump out from behind a rock and expose my ignorance. The crowds would gather and laugh, "New guy... HA HA HA ... new boy, new boy... HA HA." I'd be disgraced in front of everyone. "HA-HA, what kind of mama's boy doesn't know where to buy French fries?" They'd point and laugh and I'd stand humiliated, naked, and alone.... then I'd ask, "Where can I find a youth hostel?" "HAHA! Youth hostel? He wants the youth hostel... HA HA, BABY, BABY, he doesn't know where the youth hostel is, haha snicker, jeer..." and the crowds would laugh as I'd turn red and white and purple and green and I'd be alone and embarrassed and ashamed. Then I would start playing my guitar and a twelve-foot, 800 pound beast in a clown suit would walk over with his big feet and tell everyone, "This is his FIRST day, HA HA, look how UN-cool he is, what is he doing, he is so UN-cool..." And I would be SO UN-cool and awkward and wrong.

I fell asleep and dreamed. I dreamed that all my friends were standing on boxes and talking about me. They were talking about how great I was and how I was such a pioneer and had done such great and adventurous things. And I was there. And I was dead. And it was my funeral and I was in a box but I was there. And I sat confidently back and listened to the accolades and tales of glory and greatness and of my charm and magnetic personality. And I felt so warm and so good and so loved. It was so easy to die. No battles with monsters or awkward situations. No asking for directions. No trouble. No hassle. No effort. My mother was there and she cried and smiled and talked about what an easy baby I was. Everybody laughed and loved me. I was so loved and it was wonderful. Oh to be dead.

Then I woke up. I was still alive and in my $60 hotel room in Amsterdam.

"This is crazy," I said to myself. "It's embarrassing. It's ridiculous. Am I really such a timid, cowardly nerd? I can't sit here forever feeling sorry for myself. I have to do something."

I decided to go back to the train station. No matter what, I was going to set up my gear and start playing music. It was the only way. I just needed to get the ball rolling. I needed to meet people and move on with my radical expatriate plans. I would establish myself on the streets and that would be my in with the cool Amsterdam sub-culture.

In the morning I got up, packed up my stuff, and had breakfast. I took an ashtray from the hotel and went to the train station. I was there in no time and set up in a sunny spot in front. It was a large, unobstructed, wide-open space. I rummaged through my bag for cables and cords and set up my small, battery-powered amplifier.

"Wait." It was déjà vu, "Not now."

I persevered. I unzipped my guitar case and fumbled around for my strap. It took a few minutes to set up, tune my guitar, and plug everything in. I put down the ashtray to collect tips and loose change.

I stalled. I turned the knobs down to zero, put my ear to the body of the guitar, and played a few chords. It was a beautiful day and people were out and about. New tourists were arriving from the airport and other parts of Europe. I stood there for a while. I felt like I was seven-feet tall and dipped in neon. I didn't know what to do with myself, where to put my hands, or how to hold my body.

I fumbled around with the tuning pegs and readied myself to play. I had to do something. I had to get started.

"You can't play here."

"What?" I was taken by surprise.

A tall American guy with thick black curly hair had been watching me set up my stuff. He came over to where I was standing.

"You can't play here. The cops will arrest you and confiscate your equipment."

"Oh, really, hmm, bummer."

"They allow music in other places, just not in front of the train station. Do you have a place to stay? I can hook you up."

I followed him across town and checked into the hostel he worked for. It was seventeen dollars a night. The hostel wasn't what I was expecting, but it saved me: I met other travelers, loosened up, and got used to Amsterdam.

I thought I was cool when I left New York but I was actually a geek. I was so caught up with the idea of leaving that I never thought about what I would do once I left. But now I was in Europe and there was no turning back.

I am not an impulsive person, but the decision to leave was, although it was a good decision. I would never have left New York had I thought about it.

I got over my opening-day jitters – as embarrassing as they were – and was ready for anything.

✧ 3 ✧

I hit the streets once I got my bearings and was settled in Amsterdam. Every afternoon I was in a different square or street corner playing my guitar for loose change. Money was good and I could make as much as forty dollars an hour. I didn't play the standard folkie street music: I am a lousy singer and instrumental renditions of *American Pie* are bad (actually, any version of *American Pie* is bad). I had my wah-wah and chunked out funky grooves, blues jams, jazz tunes, and whatever else I felt like playing. Not everyone loved my music – especially drunk, fat, German tourists – but I didn't care (and it is funny to get Germans mad, *"Ve don't like ze musik."*). Playing guitar in the warm summer air was liberating and enough people threw me change to make up for the bone-headed Germans.

It didn't take long to get to know the other musicians on the street. We hung out and talked after playing music all day. One of the musicians was an older guy from India – I forget his name – he played the violin and loved talking. "You are Jewish." He told me. "Yes I am. How did you know?" He wouldn't say.

"I am Jewish too," he said. I didn't know Jews lived in India and I had never met an Indian Jew before. It never occurred to me that Jews were from anywhere except New York. He told me that his family was descended from Portuguese Jews fleeing the inquisition about 500 years ago. Cool. We were blood brothers. He made it his business to jam with me. He wasn't a good violinist, but he was a nice guy and liked to remind me that I was Jewish.

He was the first, but not the last person to ask me if I was Jewish. Everyone wanted to know. "Are you a Jew?" Other musicians asked me. Tourists and fellow travelers asked me. Everyone knew and needed to ask. I didn't think I looked Jewish but I was wrong. I looked very Jewish. It was written all over my face. I was never confronted with my Jewishness like this before. I never thought about being Jewish until I met B. I still didn't know what difference it made. B was black. Al was Italian. I was a Jew. I wasn't WHITE. But other than that? Now in Europe, everyone wanted to talk about it. "Yes I am, so what?"

In my hostel there was an evil Canadian. He was the first Canadian I met and the first Canadian I didn't like. He was one of those Canadian travelers with a Canadian flag sewn to his backpack to alert the world, "Just because I am white, rich, and English speaking is no reason to confuse me with the dirty filth south of the border." He hated me. I didn't know it. I was naive. I made a Canadian joke. He was furious. He threatened to kill me. I was shocked; in New York people are civil and can take a joke. I stared at him unsure of what to say or how to react. "Don't stare at me with those big Jewish eyes, I am going to kill you."

There it was again. Jewish. Everyone knew I was Jewish.

I don't remember what happened next, but the Canadian dropped it. Maybe he thought I was part of a vast Jewish conspiracy and he would never work again. I don't know, but he left me alone after that.

I found Hat. She was the girlfriend of a musician I worked with in New York. She wore ripped clothes and bandanas, smoked cigarettes she rolled herself, and was the stereotype of European Bohemian. She showed me the hip side of Amsterdam (beyond the tourist attractions and cheesy coffee shops). She took me to parties in illegal clubs: huge rooms with black walls, secret entrances, and passwords (it was like being at prohibition-era speakeasies, except that the music was awful and the décor was urban kitsch). She brought me to the Amsterdam art squats: abandoned buildings taken over by young artists and radicals and converted into museums, art spaces, alternative performance centers, and hangouts. I was in.

I played music on the streets every day and earned enough money for room and board. When I wasn't playing music I hung out with Hat and her Bohemian friends. After about two weeks I couldn't take it anymore. I was restless and needed to move on. As hip as Amsterdam was, it was still a small provincial town reminiscent of Boston. I needed big. I needed the European New York.

I activated my Eurorail pass and hit the road. My first stop was Köln. I spent four days there with Steve, a good friend from the Conservatory. Steve was in my first normal band in college (aside from Fat Elvis). We played nuclear bebop in our white boy jazz kind of way. We weren't that good, but we tried.

Steve left Boston a year before I did, spent time in New York, and then moved to Germany. He was living in Köln as a hip American expatriate musician. He played piano in boogie-woogie joints and spoke fluent German. I found Steve and crashed in his apartment. I spent the days listening to his massive collection of Captain Beefheart, sleeping until noon, and working out on my guitar. At nights we hit up Köln and jammed with the locals.

Köln was cool and I loved hanging out with Steve. In a different life I would have stayed in Köln forever, listening to Beefheart and jamming boogie-woogie. But I was on a mission. I had to leave.

Paris was next. After a day in a fancy pension, I searched the city for cheaper digs. I found the Aloha Youth Hostel. The Aloha Hostel was a fabulous place: four people crammed in a room and a short walk from everything. I found two-dollar bottles of wine, moldy cheese, coffee, baguettes, and became French.

On the train ride from Köln to Paris I realized that the inter-city journeys were a lot longer than I had anticipated. The little lines and gaps on the map don't translate into real distances until you are actually traveling them. On the train I stared out the windows and looked at the walls. I was bored out of my mind. I needed something to read. I stared at my fingernails, examined my cuticles, read candy wrappers, fiddled with my watch, and counted trees and small buildings as they passed by my window. I searched the train for a newspaper. No luck, everything was in French. I couldn't do this on my next trip. I needed a book. Reading was the only way to survive the long trips. I soon realized that it was the only way to get through the long days too. I was not interested in sight seeing, I was on tour to find people, escape New York, and figure out what Henry Miller was talking about.

As luck would have it, someone left a book in my fancy French hotel room. It was a cheesy John Irving novel but it didn't matter. Once I started reading I couldn't stop. I was hooked and I read at least ten books that summer. I found books in hostels, on trains, in used English-only shops, and traded with other travelers. I read all the apocalyptic novels like *Brave New World*, *1984*, *Fahrenheit 451*. I read the *Unbearable Lightness of Being* and Kafka in preparation for my journeys East. I read James Joyce and *Naked Lunch* – and a bunch of other stuff too. The two books that had the biggest impact on me that summer were the *Autobiography of Malcolm X* and *On the Road* by Jack Kerouac.

I discovered *Malcolm X* in Paris. The Aloha Hostel had a daily lockout from nine-to-five (this is standard practice in many hostels, they can clean the rooms undisturbed and it cuts down on crime). Since I couldn't sit in my room all day, I walked the streets and sometimes played guitar outside the Centre Pompidou. Most days I ended up near Notre Dame.

Shakespeare and Company is an English language bookshop across the Seine from Notre Dame. I heard a rumor that James Joyce hung out there and wrote. Being a hip expatriate like Joyce, I decided to hang out at Shakespeare and Company too. It was my home in the daytime, my refuge from hot Paris days when the Aloha barred me from my room. I settled into a routine and every morning I walked to Shakespeare and Company munching on cheese and croissants. I read the books on the shelves for free and one of them was the *Autobiography of Malcolm X*.

Malcolm X blew my mind. He was so clear and in touch with his identity. He stood for the same things B stood for, except that he wasn't an early nineties feminist poet, he was the real deal. He lived for an ideal, he was consistent, he wasn't afraid to say what he thought, he was honest, he was willing to admit when he was mistaken, and he died for what he believed in. Malcolm X didn't apologize for who he was. He was who he was: if it bothered you, too bad.

I wanted to be Malcolm X. I read his book every morning and hit the streets in the afternoons. I walked and walked. I walked a few miles a day and lost twenty pounds. I thought about Malcolm X when I walked. I couldn't stop thinking about him. I wanted to be just like him.

But I wasn't anything like him. I didn't believe in anything. I didn't have a cause. I didn't have an identity. I was a nice Jewish boy from suburban New Jersey and I fancied myself an urban hipster expatriate wanderer musician. Whatever that means. I think it is code for self-absorbed, pretentious, looking for meaning, afraid of the consequences, empty-headed Jewish kid without a clue and no idea where to start.

Malcolm's rants swirled through my head. I tried to process his ideas via my middleclass suburban Jewish filter. I needed someone to be mad at. There were plenty of people to be mad at: weren't most American Jews sellouts? I was. "Man. These American Jews with their Anglicized last names and nose jobs man. Fight the power."

Silly. I was silly.

But Malcolm X awakened something in me. He was authentic. I needed to be authentic. Who did I want to be? Why did so many people in Amsterdam ask me if I was Jewish? Someone was sending me signs. I first thought about my identity in New York. It caught up with me in Europe. I ignored it. For the rest of the summer Jews and Judaism popped up at random and unexpected times, especially as I moved into the newly liberated east. I put it on a back shelf and filed it away. At the end of the summer it would be the final motivation to get me to Israel and the driving force behind the new direction my life would take. But more about that later.

I read *On the Road* after I finished *Malcolm X*. *On the Road* is a quasi-mystical religious experience about the search for the ultimate *it* – the meaning and reason for everything. The book summed up so much of what I was thinking about but couldn't articulate. I wanted *it*: that magic, insane, mad, out-of-this-world feeling that zaps you when you slip beyond the mundane. The primal fire and energy of life – when all hell breaks loose and the feeling is palpable – like when the band is raging, your team is winning, or the conversation is pregnant with intensity. I wanted *it* all the time. Sometimes I had it. But *it* always ended, no matter how high I got.

Maybe that was the reason I escaped New York. I tasted *it* in Köln and in the energy of Paris, but I wanted it all the time. It wasn't enough. I thought about the last time I really had it.

Botz and I worked in a number of different bands together. Our main gig was the Blues Posse: a raunchy blues-based three piece. It featured our other roommate (B's predecessor) on bass and vocals, Botz on drums, and me on guitar, harmonica, occasional vocals, weird noises and comic relief.

Our landlord rented us her basement in Carol Gardens in Brooklyn. It was a dumpy little room and we soundproofed the walls with carpets. The carpets stunk but we managed. The room was packed chockablock with instruments, amps, speakers, cables, random electronics, and recording equipment. We spent a few hours a night in the space working through revamped versions of old blues standards, originals, and open-ended funk grooves. When the Blues Posse wasn't practicing, we used the space for other projects and to record new music.

The Blues Posse's style was open-ended and loose; we left huge spaces in our music for extended improvisations. We never played a song the same way twice. It was not unusual for the songs to bleed into each other when we played live. We were not a clean, Dead-inspired jam band. We were a nasty, gritty, in-your-face blues unit with fuzz, slide, and coupled with the sophistication and over-playing of recent music school graduates. We were not angry or punk – just loud – and we had a sense of humor (we often switched instruments and played cheesy renditions of Broadway show tunes). We were a trio, vocals were kept to a minimum, and as the guitarist I took most of the solos.

My solos were a mess of energy, colors, and textures. I experimented with space and sounds, or got bored and just played fast. I was not a front man and the other guys were not my backup band – it didn't work that way – we were a unified outfit.

And Botz could read my mind. I never looked at him to indicate a change, new texture, or idea. He instinctively understood where I was headed (or where he was sending me) and we arrived at the same place without plan or discussion. It just happened.

A few of my friends from college were from Hoboken and big on the local music scene there. They got the Blues Posse a gig at Boo-Boo's, a small bar one block from the PATH station boasting live music every night of the week. We rocked our first gig – the locals went nuts – and we were invited back once a month. It became our regular haunt and on the weekends it was always packed. We usually started our first set at 11:30 and played until two or three in the morning. We played other places too, especially around Manhattan, but Boo-Boo's was special.

The band was loose by the end of the first set (we played three a night). The room was packed and dark. The wait staff pushed through people crowded around tables and crammed into corners. We launched into an extended jam. I soloed. We moved through space and swamps and stepped off the levee in hip-waders and rubber boots. We were knee deep in funk. The energy was palpable. I stepped outside and the music raged. I watched from the rafters, up with the beat lighting rig and speakers. My fingers moved and the guitar played itself. Stale beer, napkins, and little plastic straws stuck to the floors under the hundreds of feet in the room. Magic. I never wanted it to end. I was in a parallel universe, a zone reserved for someone else. The audience was there too. The endless talking and flirting stopped for a minute. We were in a different dimension. The people at the bar boogied. The dudes in the back stared over their beers. The room was alive in unity, a mass moving together to an unknown zone one step beyond the limits of everyday. And it was bigger than all of us. Somehow the sum total of the experience outweighed our individual contributions. One plus one equals three – I think they call it gestalt.

This was *it*. I never wanted it to end. I could spend eternity on that stage, behind my guitar and in the zone.

The high was real and intense. It was a place I ended up and wasn't prepared for, but once I got there I never wanted to leave.

And then it was time to go home. The staff wanted to count their tips and close up. We packed up our gear and drove back to Brooklyn alone. We dumped our stuff at our rehearsal space and went out for breakfast before going to bed. We never discussed it yet we knew we were in a place most people dream about and sometimes get to by accident.

At breakfast we got distracted with cheap eggs, hash browns, and black pepper. Botz extolled the virtues of coffee, New York, Italian delicatessens, fresh mozzarella, pasta fagioli, and why we needed to spend more time in Sheepshead Bay. I went home and crashed. The *it* was gone.

4

For most of the summer I zigzagged across Europe – sometimes south to Spain or north to Sweden – but always moving east. I wasn't sure how I was going to get back. (I didn't think that far in advance. At some point I needed to return to Amsterdam to catch my flight home.) But for the time being it was east – keep moving east – into the former Soviet bloc, closer to Asia and the Middle East, always east. By mid-summer I was in Prague.

I took a train after a two-week stint in sophisticated, modern Sweden, heading south towards Prague with a layover in Berlin. I got off the train in Berlin to look around. I had thought about staying there for a few days, but once I stepped into the station I decided against it. The energy of Berlin rubbed me the wrong way. I didn't dig the vibe. After three hours I was back on the train and headed for Prague.

Prague was alive in the summer of 1993. It was new, fresh from its Soviet days, and slowly shaking off the shackles of oppression and a planned economy. Václav Havel was president – the hipsters and artists had taken over – and there was talk of inviting Frank Zappa to be the Minister of Culture. Entrepreneurial young Czechs squatted in government buildings and converted them into bars, jazz joints, restaurants, and art spaces.

Every free spirited, left-leaning, effected Bohemian was in liberated Eastern Europe and Prague was the Mecca. In addition to fly-by-night tourists like me, there were a good number of young Americans and others who moved to Prague to live cheap (you could get a place at the time for $40 a month) and discover themselves.

I arrived in the morning. The hostel I found was a university dorm converted into cheap housing for travelers. It was at the top of a hill, next to Eastern Europe's largest football stadium, on the same side of the river as Prague's famous castle. The dorm complex was massive. It was a system of six concrete communist-era buildings ("Come Comrade, we build housing for the workers.") – each housed a few hundred people – surrounding an enormous parking lot that no one used.

My room cost six dollars a night. For six dollars I got a large room (that was technically for two people but I had it to myself most of the time), access to the massive community shower, and a beer. A small "café" was set up near the building that housed the office and check-in; I went there every day for my beer and to sit around. In Prague in those days the radio and restaurants only played three albums: the *Grease* soundtrack, *Saturday Night Fever*, and *Lionel Richie's Greatest Hits*. This was the music of freedom.

I spent my days wandering the city. I read a few Czech authors before arriving to prepare for my visit (Kafka was a crybaby – "nobody likes me, I am just a bug"), but nothing hit me like *On the Road* or *Malcolm X*. It didn't matter. I walked around and thought about life. When I wasn't walking around, I was at Joe's American Bar.

Joe's was at the bottom of the massive hill that descended from the stadium to the river, ending at the famous Charles Bridge. It was a small place run by Americans and designed to attract English-speaking travelers. They served Czech beer, Czech-style Mexican food (i.e. beans and rotten lettuce), and played music other than *Saturday Night Fever*. I went there every day, ate tacos, and drank the Czech version of Budweiser.

Everyone at Joe's was just like me, lost American hipsters in Europe. Most of them were looking for something. They were musicians, poets, painters, and loafers. Many were living in Prague – and not traveling like I was – to take advantage of the cheap lifestyle and abundant opportunity. None of them were talented enough to make it in New York – or any major center – but in a place like Prague they could get steady work, which they did. I hung out with them and got to know them. They were cool people. I decided to move to Prague after my travels.

I discovered a different *it* in Prague. A quiet *it*, the opposite of a raging band, but just as intense. It was the *it* of a great conversation or an all night road trip.

The Blues Posse sometimes had gigs in Western Pennsylvania (an eight-hour drive from our apartment in Brooklyn). Botz and I drove – my car packed with equipment – and our bass player took the bus. We drove at night, listened to AM radio, dug Billy Preston, talked about life, and got off on the road.

The first time we made the trip, the highway stunk. It was the smell of dead animals, garbage, and sulfur. It was horrible. The smell wouldn't go away. We opened the windows, played with the heater, blew the fan – nothing got rid of it. We passed trucks, vans, a garbage truck, farms, urban areas – and the smell was still there. We passed a flatbed carrying nothing. The smell was gone.

Strange.

We pulled off the highway to get coffee. "Only mild, light brown coffee in Pennsylvania. You will notice that the coffee gets weaker and weaker the further you get from New York. We'll have to drink twice as much to get the same effect. The problem is that the peristalsis is twice as intense. That will cost time." Botz smoked. We ate eggs, hash browns, black pepper, and toast and got back on the highway.

The smell was back. We played with the heater and windows again. The smell wouldn't go away. Up ahead I noticed the empty flatbed we passed earlier. We passed it again. The smell went away. "Botz, the truck is carrying smell." And it was.

We made a number of trips to Western Pennsylvania and they were always the same: trucks carrying smell, weak coffee, hash browns, black pepper, AM radio, and talking. We talked a lot. We talked about music, Zappa, New York, life, women, Botz's divorce, marriage, his cat with six fingers, fiber, the wonders of the digestive system, and how Ringo is really a great drummer. "No one appreciates him except people who don't know any better. Check out *Dear Prudence* or the backwards snare on *Strawberry Fields*. The man is a genius."

The highway crossed the entire length of the state. I drove and Botz fiddled with the radio. "Julius Sumner Miller makes me dig physics. I love his hair." We peaked.

Ringo Starr and Julius Sumner Miller were at the epicenter of the universe. I slipped into the zone. Beyond the band and the music, *it* was a tangible reality I could touch in conversation too. "One day I am taking this highway all the way to the other coast," I said. I never wanted it to end.

We turned off the highway and followed the roads through the forest. We made a left onto a dirt road. Soon we were in a farmhouse eating breakfast and talking about the weather. It was over.

I ran out of money in Prague. I needed a MasterCard. MasterCard was the only card the money exchange places accepted. I only had Visa. I don't know why the Czechs took MasterCard but not Visa, but that's how it was. Prague in the summer of 1993 was still a developing city.

I wanted to stay in Prague forever. My experience was magical. I found my niche. But I had to move on. I went to Berlin to meet a friend from New York. Big mistake. After Berlin I spent time in Krakow, Budapest, and Turkey. It was in Turkey that I decided to go to Israel.

I splurged: I spent $150 and flew from Budapest to Istanbul. I considered taking the train, but it was a 24-hour ride through Romania during times of unrest and not so long after the coup and murder of the Ceaușescus. I called the American embassy in Bucharest. They told me that the train ride was safe so long as I didn't fall asleep. I decided to fly, what was there to see in Romania anyway?

I landed in Istanbul and took a bus from the airport into town. On the bus I met an Australian tourist. He was a typical Australian. He had been traveling for seven years and would travel another seven before returning home. He knew where the hostels were (in Istanbul they were in the Old City). He got a job in one – like all Australians do – in order to extend his travels. I followed him to the Old City, near the famous mosques and carpet dealers, and got a room.

I spent a few days in Istanbul, but I was lonely and there wasn't much to do. I was amazed by the cement slabs in the middle of the main streets, at how weak the currency was (I exchanged $100 and became a millionaire for the first time), and how third world everything seemed.

It was my first time in a non-western country. The post-communist cities of Eastern Europe were backwards but exciting in spite of the bland, toothless locals. Turkey was a different vibe and unlike anything I experienced, especially the bathhouses, hookah joints, street side shoe-shine boys, and carpets. Carpets were for sale everywhere.

After about three days I decided to travel to central Turkey. I took the bus. Turkish buses are insane: the windows are sealed shut, the air conditioner is pumping, and all the passengers smoke nonstop. My lungs went black and pasty just sitting there. We traveled over the massive bridge that spans two continents and I was in Asia for the first time in my life.

I arrived in central Turkey and got off the bus in Goreme. (Goreme is the main village I visited in central Turkey, the region is called Kapadokia). The area looks like the surface of the moon: tall, odd-shaped mounds of limestone hollowed out a thousand years ago by Christians in hiding. People still live in the limestone mounds. The towns are built on hillsides. The buildings are just façade set up in front of manmade caves. It is a wild place. I found a hostel (also a cave). The hostel was full but had a bar they never used. They let me sleep in the bar. I didn't mind and relished having a private space.

I met a few tourists from England and New York. They were pseudo-intellectual art types and in their thirties. They were touring the backwoods of Turkey to avoid the lame college kids traveling in Western Europe and on the beaches in Greece. I liked them. We hiked, argued with the carpet sellers, and ate tons of eggplant. The eggplant gave us terrible gas. It was a blessing we spent most of our time outdoors.

Israel announced the Oslo Accords while I was in Goreme: a deal with the Palestinians was imminent. I thought this was cool and it would be cool to be in Israel for the historic signing. It was late in August and I was aware that Rosh Hashanah was coming up too. I called my mother to get the exact date. I thought it would be cool to be in Israel for Rosh Hashanah. I wasn't interested in going to synagogue – I hadn't done that in years – I wanted to be in Israel for the holiday, even if I just went to a kibbutz and got drunk.

I had ten days to get to Israel. I asked around and found out about a boat that went from Athens to Israel, stopping at Rhodes and Cypress along the way. I decided to catch that boat. I said goodbye to my new artsy friends and took a bus to the southern Turkish coast. I hung out there for a day. The next day I spent $22 to ride the hydrofoil to Rhodes. There was a slower boat that only cost $10, but how often did I get to ride a hydrofoil? I saw a hippie couple waiting for the cheap boat. I watched them from the deck as we pushed off from the dock.

The boat pulled into Rhodes. I got off and went through Greek customs. The paranoid boarder control seized my passport and kept it in a box until I left the country. I found a room in town and spent a day walking around wondering what it was going to be like in Israel. I saw a building that once belonged to the Jewish community. It was abandoned. Jews don't use it anymore. I hung out and waited for my big boat. I tried to speak to the lady who ran my hostel, but she only spoke Greek.

The boat cost $99. It was going to take two full days to get to Israel. The trip had an 8-hour layover in Cypress with time to get off the boat and look around. My ticket was the cheapest they sold; it gave me access to the deck and nothing else. I could sit on the deck, sleep on the deck, talk to the other people on the deck, but I wasn't allowed inside the boat – and especially not the casino. I was allowed inside to use the bathrooms, but the boat's crew wasn't happy about it. I didn't care. Sleeping on the deck was glamorous.

There were a few others staying on the deck with me including the hippie couple I saw the day before from the deck of the hydrofoil. They sat down next to me and set up shop: we were going to be one big happy family. They set up their sleeping bags, camping gear, survival kit, and trail mix. I didn't have a sleeping bag. I used a sweatshirt as a blanket and my bag as a pillow.

We hung out. There was nothing to do – especially once the boat was in the open sea – so we talked. We talked nonstop for two days. The hippie couple – Kofi and Rebecca – was from New Jersey. Kofi grew up in Rockaway, ten minutes away from my parents' house. We bonded. His parents were in the Peace Corps and living in Ghana when he was born – hence his cool name. Rebecca, his girlfriend, wasn't as exciting. They met in Israel and went to Bulgaria to campout in the woods. They were going back to Israel to work on a kibbutz before going back to the States for grad school.

Kofi and I hit it off immediately. I was a well-read, thinking, pretentious talking machine (and I had six months of travel behind me). Everything oozed out. All my thoughts about life, religion, Malcolm X, *it* – everything I was thinking about that summer came out in a quasi-Jewish, spiritual, artistic torrent. Kofi dug it all. We talked and talked and drove poor Rebecca crazy, she couldn't keep up. I was reading a copy of *Naked Lunch* (the *Beat* classic by William S. Burroughs) I borrowed from one of the people I met in Goreme. I was fascinated by his ideas about religion and drugs, particularly his thoughts about Indian medicine men taking peyote and seeing visions. We talked about that. I wanted to find my identity and see visions. Maybe religion and God were just energy or a psychological state. You could reach it if you focused and worked on it (not that I had the patience to). And somehow it was Jewish.

Kofi was all about psychological states. "Burroughs is right." He told me about psychology, drugs, art, music, and God. He thought they were all trains to the same place.

The emotional flow of our talks was intense. It was real. It was *it* and it was representative of my headspace: I spent the entire summer traveling, reading, thinking, and walking around. Being Jewish was on my brain: Europe put it there, from the questions in Amsterdam to Malcolm X in Paris to the Jewish ghost towns of the East. I wanted it all: life, love, and the meaning and essence of everything. I was in the zone. I was ready. I was on the verge of a breakthrough. I just had no idea what it could be.

We talked like that for two days. I didn't bother getting off the boat in Cypress to look around. There was too much to talk about.

I woke up on the second day and we were in Haifa just off the Israeli coast, in the harbor waiting for permission to dock. It was five o'clock in the morning. I stared at the mountains along the shore. Israel. I was paralyzed. Home. The Motherland. What was this? I was overcome by a wave of emotion and a weird sentimentality. Odd. I needed to get off the boat and kiss the ground. Why? Israel was not a place I thought about before. Why did I feel connected? It was very strange.

Kofi and Rebecca packed up and made plans to go straight to Jerusalem. They were going to a kibbutz. I decided to follow them and see if I could crash with them for free.

We got off the boat and went through Israeli customs. Rebecca said there was a bus for Jerusalem leaving in ten minutes. We ran. We ran through the streets of Haifa. We weren't going to make it. I was exhausted and with my guitar, amp, and stuff I couldn't keep up. Rebecca screamed at me. "Hurry up. You are going to blow this for us. Why are you following us? Come on!"

We made it. I couldn't fall asleep on the bus. I was too excited. I looked out the windows. I looked at the other people on the bus, the soldiers and girls carrying M-16s. Two and a half hours later we were in the Central Bus Station in Jerusalem.

I got off the bus. It was hot. A girl greeted me as I fumbled with my stuff. She was wearing a sweater and long skirt. "Are you Jewish?" "Yes." I was uneasy. I didn't like the question. It didn't bother me in Amsterdam, but here it was weird. "I work for a youth hostel in the Old City." Nothing unusual. "It is free if you are Jewish." Strange. "Here is a card." I took the card. I thought she was a Moonie.

Rebecca called the kibbutz. I couldn't stay with them; it wasn't going to work out. "Stay at the free place in the Old City." She said.

"No way. I can't go there. It is a cult. They will brainwash me. Not for me. No thank you. I will figure something out."

"What are you afraid of?" What was I afraid of? "You haven't stopped talking about Judaism and spirituality and medicine men. You and Kofi drove me crazy. Now you are afraid? Loser." She was right. "Go. What will they do to you? Give you free food and talk about God? Go."

She was right. I was a big baby.

We said goodbye. I got directions and walked to the Old City. I wasn't prepared for what would happen to me.

✧ 6 ✧

Jerusalem's Old City is a maze. It is easy to get lost there. If you don't know your way around you can end up in neighborhoods you don't want to be in. Stone, walls, camels, donkeys, ladies handing out red string, Arabs selling Middle Eastern bagels and pita; the Old City is no place to just show up and look around.

But that is what I did. I had the card the girl gave me at the bus station; it had a map on the back. I followed the directions and found the hostel. The hostel was locked (they had a lockout similar to the Aloha Hostel in Paris). I looked in and saw someone mopping the floors. I knocked. He saw me and noticed my guitar and rig. He let me in and locked up my stuff in the office.

"Do you want to meet my rebbe?" He asked.

"Ok," I didn't know what a rebbe was. I guessed it was some type of rabbi or something. The janitor made me nervous. I was here against my better judgment: the girl at the bus station gave me the jitters, but Rebecca convinced me to check it out. Now I was going to meet the *rebbe*. I was terrified. The youth hostel was a front for a cult – even the janitor was in on it – I was lost. I was going to die. They were going to make me drink Kool-Aid and do calisthenics at three in the morning and eat pasta and fast and then try to cram God into my head – what was I going to do?

I followed the janitor through the Old City streets until we reached a storefront synagogue. We went in and he introduced me to the rebbe. The rebbe was not much older than me. He had a massive beard and crazy sores on his hands.

"What's your name?" The rebbe asked me. I told him. "No man, your *name*?" He meant my Hebrew name. I tried to pronounce it for him. "You mean Tzvi." He said. "Yeah, I guess that is what I mean." I looked around his storefront synagogue. There was a basket of hats near the door. The hats looked like the colorful fezzes the Red Hot Chili Peppers wore on their first album. The hats were cool and stylish. "What are these cool hats?" I asked. "Those are *yarmulkes* Tzvi." No way. Yarmulkes, but they were cool – not round little beanies – the brothers and B's friends in Brooklyn didn't have hats as cool as these. "Can I try one on?" "Sure, Tzvi, enjoy." I put one on. I felt multicultural, hip, earthy, ethnic, everything – yet it was Jewish – this was going to be cool. I looked around the room. I looked in the mirror. I loved my new headgear.

I was starving. The rebbe had a plate of cookies sitting on a table. "Can I have a cookie? I am starving." I asked. And it was true, I was starving, I hadn't eaten since the day before on the boat – we didn't have time running through the streets of Haifa and I didn't think about it after we arrived in Jerusalem. "Sure, Tzvi, you can have a cookie." I took a cookie.

"Jews say a *blessing* before they eat a cookie," he said, "will you say a blessing with me, Tzvi?"

"Ok."

The rebbe was insane. I could see it in his eyes. He was out of his mind – he was a deranged religious lunatic – a psychopathic manipulator. I was going to die. We mumbled a few Hebrew words together, word-by-word.

"Amen." He said Amen. I said Amen. I ate the cookie. It wasn't very good.

He offered me a glass of water. "Would you like a glass of water? You are probably very thirsty." I was. "Jews say a *blessing* before they drink a glass of water, Tzvi." Oh no. We mumbled Hebrew words again, word-by-word, as he instructed. We finished and I took a sip. I was overwhelmed.

"Tzvi?"

"Yes."

"Would you like to put on *Tefillin*?" What? "It is Jewish Leather."

What was I going to do?

First, I was going to find Rebecca and kill her, she was the one who talked me into this. Then I was going to kill the janitor, but not until after he brought me back to the hostel so I could get my stuff. What was going on and why was this rebbe torturing me with his in-your-face Judaism? What did I do to deserve this? I just wanted a free place to crash, cheap food, and to be in Israel for Rosh Hashanah. After the holiday I wanted to go back to Amsterdam so I could catch my flight home.

The rebbe took out the *Tefillin*: black boxes and leather straps. "Roll up your sleeve." He was going to take blood. I knew it. I was in for it.

I tried to calm down. "This is going to make a great story to tell Al and Botz, they are going to love this." I thought. Al will laugh for hours, "Haha, Jerusalem in Jerusalem (I can hear his dad now) and Jerusalem is wearing black leather, Jewish leather. Hahahaha." I was not going to panic. I was going to stay calm. Everything was going to be ok.

The rebbe took the second leather box and put it on my head. "Can you read Hebrew, Tzvi?"

"No. I mean I know what some of the letters are but not all of them and I can't really read so well, you know how it is."

"You need to say the *Shema* when you put on *Tefillin*. Do you know what the *Shema* is, Tzvi?" I sort of did, but I couldn't really remember and I certainly couldn't read it. He handed me a little card, "read this." It was Hebrew words transliterated into English. I mumbled. After about five minutes the rebbe took off the *Tefillin* and I was free to go.

"What are you doing for Rosh Hashanah, Tzvi?"

"I am not really sure, I am going to try and find some place to hang out I guess."

"So you will spend it in Jerusalem. You will eat lunch with me. This is my address. We start at one. Do not be late." I didn't know what to say. I was too afraid to tell him to take a hike, but I wanted to – there was no way I was going near this mad insane out-of-his-mind manipulative freak ever again. Instead I just smiled and nodded. I looked like someone with a lobotomy.

"Can I keep the yarmulke?" I asked.

"No, Tzvi, they are for sale." I didn't want to pay for it so I left.

What was I going to do? Why did I listen to Rebecca? Why didn't I stay in Haifa and hang out there? What was I doing in Jerusalem? I still had a few hours before I was allowed back into the hostel to get my stuff or check in. The janitor disappeared. I decided to walk around; I walked around every other city I visited, why should Jerusalem be any different?

I wandered until I saw the Western Wall. I stopped. I felt apprehensive. I couldn't walk up to it. Strange. I needed to buy a yarmulke first. I had to own a yarmulke if I was going to touch the Western Wall. I thought about it. "What kind of Jew comes to Israel and doesn't own a yarmulke?" Right. "But what about the paper yarmulkes the Wall security staff is giving out?" Those are for gentiles, Jews own their own. I decided to buy one of those hip, colorful, Red Hot Chili Pepper fezzes that the rebbe had, except that I was not going back to buy one from him. No way.

I wandered on. Soon I was in a different part of the Old City, far away from the tourists and fancy buildings. The walls were covered with colorful graffiti. The people walking on the streets looked different – they were Arabs – the area reminded me of Istanbul.

I kept walking. The locals were looking at me funny. I was oblivious. I was on another international adventure and my mind was mulling over the events of the day; the rebbe, his invitation, the leather, the yarmulke, the hostel – I was in a different universe.

I saw a group of Arab kids playing soccer. "What are you doing here?" They asked me.

"Nothing." Really, I was just wandering and thinking about life.

"Are you looking for the hospital?" There was a hospital in the area, though I didn't know that.

"No."

"You shouldn't be here, you can get killed." Killed. Now that was scary. I didn't want to get killed. Killed is bad. "Follow us, we'll show you how to get out of here." They took me to one of the gates of the Old City and pointed the way to Ben Yehuda Street, the central tourist area. I thanked them and spent the rest of the day wandering around Ben Yehuda Street, looking in the stores, and eating falafel.

I went back to the free hostel in the evening. The guy running the check-in was normal and pleasant. "What are you doing in Israel?" He asked.

"I don't really know. I have been traveling all summer."

"How long are you staying in Israel for?"

"I don't know."

"What do you want to do while you are here?"

"I don't know." I didn't want to tell him that this is what I had been doing all summer: bumming around, reading, walking, and talking to random people. I wasn't looking to change my routine.

"You can stay here. It is free, except on Shabbos and then it will cost you fifteen shekels but that is a bargain because we set you up for two meals and third meal is here."

I didn't know what he was talking about. I knew there was Jewish Sabbath, but only old people called it "Shabbos." What did he mean "set you up for meals?" Someone was going to feed me, like the rebbe's lunch invite? And what is a "Third Meal?"

Whatever. Free sounded good and fifteen shekels wasn't much money (at the time it was five dollars). I checked in. The other guests were normal. We hung out and talked. I was going to be ok. I didn't need to stress: nobody confiscated my passport, I was able to sleep the whole night (they didn't wake me up to exercise), and I didn't drink any Kool-Aid.

Maybe I would brave a meal with the rebbe too.

7

There was a yeshiva near my hostel. They offered a free breakfast if you stayed for a class. I went. The breakfast was Israeli salad, milk in a bag, fake cornflakes, a hard-boiled egg, cottage cheese, and yogurt: not as cool as the food I ate in Paris, but free and I didn't complain. The classes were better. They were challenging, spiritual, intelligent, religious, Jewish, and unapologetic. They taught about God and science, faith and belief, psychology, inner conflict, morality, apathy, and marriage.

I hung out with the people I met in the classes at night. We talked about Jews, Judaism, and the things we were learning. Everyone was Jewish. The other students were Jewish. The teachers were Jewish. The people in the bars were Jewish. Even the waiters, bartenders, cops, and bus drivers were Jewish. The whole country was Jewish. I loved not being a minority. Judaism was all I talked about. All my experiences, thoughts, ideas, and identity were coming together. It was a cosmic meeting. I was excited and nervous.

The teachers claimed the ideas they taught were authentic. Were they? I didn't care. The claim was enough for me. I wanted to be authentic. I thought about my life in New York. It was a thousand years ago: I was lost there and I looked for answers. I looked in books, art, music, the band, Prospect Park, and the knish shops on Delancey Street. I never thought the answers were Jewish. I didn't know any better. I ran away looking for something. Maybe this was it. I thought about my first day in Israel – the girl at the bus station, the Wall, and the rebbe – what was I so afraid of?

My first week in Israel went by in a flash and then it was Rosh Hashanah. Rosh Hashanah in Israel is like Christmas in America: the whole country shuts down and everything stops. What do Christians do in Israel on the Jewish holidays? Do they feel stupid like Jews do in America? Do they eat Chinese food and watch movies? I thought about this. I really loved not being a minority.

I was set up with families for the Rosh Hashanah meals. "All the restaurants and stores are closed," the guy at the hostel claimed. "If you don't let us set you up with a family you will starve." I was game. I like free food. Earlier that summer a Swedish farm girl took me to her home in central Sweden. Her mother cooked me dinner. It was elk. It was the only elk I ever ate. It tasted like brisket (are the Swedes Jewish?). Her father was a hunter. He shot the elk himself. If I could eat elk in Sweden I could eat with Jewish families in Jerusalem.

I was sent to a small apartment in the Old City with another guy from the hostel. The host spoke broken English. It was weird, but our host was a nice guy. He tried to teach us a lesson in English. It didn't work. "You see, blah blah blah, a GOY, blah blah blah, GOY, blah blah blah Rosh Hashanah, GOY. Do you get it?" I didn't get it. I am sure he meant well. "Thank you for letting us eat in your home with your family," I said. He didn't understand. We smiled and shook hands. It was awkward. We left. I went back to the hostel and went to bed.

I slept late the next morning; the hostel didn't have a lockout on Rosh Hashanah. That afternoon I went to the rebbe for lunch. By this point I was used to Israel, Jews, and people talking about religion. He wasn't so crazy or intimidating. I could leave if he bothered me. I didn't. He fed me well and we hung out. He was a drummer and he played the bongos. He had a lot of books. His kids didn't stop screaming. I liked him.

The next few weeks were nice. I ate my free breakfast, took the obligatory class, wandered around the rest of the day, hung out at night, and talked about Judaism. I thought about leaving: I needed to get to Amsterdam to catch my flight home. I decided not to deal with it. Living in Israel was cheap and I was enjoying myself – why leave?

The holiday of Simchas Torah was at the end of September that year and I had been in Israel for a month. The streets were packed. There were mobs of people dancing and singing. The city was festive and alive. The bars were closed so there wasn't much else to do. I wandered around the Jewish Quarter with my new friends. They wanted to dance at one of the yeshivas. OK. Why not?

The yeshiva we went to was small. It was rundown, the walls were lined with books – many of them used, beat, and well loved – and the room was packed. We walked in. The music was deafening. I was immediately consumed by the dancing mob. I don't know how many people were crammed into that tiny space but it seemed like a lot. And they were all men; there were no women dancing in the yeshiva.

Two guys grabbed my hands a pulled me into a dancing circle. Around and around we went. The music was blaring, the dancing was intense, it was hot in the room, I was sweating (everyone was), and the place stunk. My circle was just one of many going around at a breakneck speed. We were moving, running, sweating, and yet packed together and squashed. If you fell you were dead. A few guys carrying Torah scrolls were dancing in the center of the room. They had big sheets on their shoulders and over their heads. They were dancing with the Torah scrolls, spinning in circles, sweating, and the focus of all the action.

Someone from the crowd – I guess one of the leaders – grabbed me and pulled me into the center. He threw a *tallis* (the big sheet) over my head and handed me a Torah scroll. It weighed a ton. I stood there in the middle as the swirling mass of men went around and around. Ecstasy and joy, loud music, noise, and celebration: they were with me in the center of the circle. It was hard to dance because the Torah was so heavy so I just sort of moved around, sweat, and took in the experience.

In the middle of all this – as I danced with the heavy Torah scroll – I realized something incredible. It was about the music and I was surprised I hadn't noticed it earlier. Maybe I hadn't noticed because the music was so loud. All of the music – and I mean *all* of it – was coming from men singing, stamping on the floor, and nothing else. There was no band, no instruments, no sound system, no DJ, no electronics, no acoustic guitars, no nothing. I was floored. This was my tribe. The experience was primal. It was tribal.

Think about it.

There were no women in the room – only men – we danced and it was intense, loud, authentic, and unpretentious. It never occurred to me that Judaism could be this way. What happened to the boring services? Where was the inane, empty sermon? Was Judaism really this cool?

I felt like Alex Haley. In *Roots* (the story tracing his family's history) he goes to Gambia and finds his tribe. He was home. Israel was my Gambia. The Jewish people were my tribe. I was home too. We had our tribal customs, dress, and wild traditions. We danced with our books. We were able to go wild without a band, women, or any of the things considered essential when Western people celebrate. We were real, even if we wore conservative suits and black hats.

I gave the Torah and *tallis* to someone else and danced for the rest of the night. I didn't want to leave. I had to stay in Israel. I had to understand. This was why I left New York and wandered Europe. I was looking for something. This was it. I was not going to let it go.

My experience on Simchas Torah convinced me to stick around for a while. I found everything I was searching for in Israel – ethnic identity, *it* – everything. In the classes

I learned a philosophy about life that was consistent and Jewish. I didn't have plans. I didn't have a job, an apartment, commitments, or anything back home. The only thing I had was my ticket for a flight from Amsterdam to New York and it was valid for another six months.

I asked around and found out that I was able to move into the dorm of the yeshiva I danced at on Simchas Torah. They wouldn't ask for money upfront, but I had to make an agreement on good faith that I would pay them back. I was expected to attend classes and be a part of the yeshiva in exchange for food and housing, which was fine with me.

I moved in and I was put in a room with five guys. They were about my age and from England, Australia, St. Louis, India, and Russia. I liked them. There were serious and got up early to pray and get to classes on time. They tolerated my late nights and sleeping in.

I dug the classes. The teachers were open-minded, worldly, and knowledgeable. The classes were sophisticated, challenging, and philosophically mature. Their approach was very different from the fluff I was taught in Hebrew school (empty bible stories the teachers didn't believe and treated as a joke). My new teachers took the material seriously. They were well read and knowledgeable. Most importantly, they believed what they were teaching. I noticed when I visited them in their homes that they put into practice the values they preached in class. This was cool.

The teachers encouraged debate in class: they were happy when we didn't accept what they told us at face value. They enjoyed the challenge of direct confrontation. One of my roommates let me borrow his translation of the Torah. I read it cover to cover and in class asked questions based on what I read.

As the days and weeks went by I enjoyed being in yeshiva more and more. I dug being Jewish, what I was learning, and the whole Israel/Jewish vibe. My mother sent me a coat and a few more shirts from home. I grew my beard. I got new pants (the pair I wore all summer were ripped to shreds). I got a real yarmulke in addition to the Chili Pepper fez I bought after first meeting the rebbe. I stopped doing things on Shabbos (and I started calling it Shabbos) and I stopped eating foods that were obviously not kosher, not that I knew where to get shrimp or pork in Jerusalem.

The more I learned, the more I understood how ignorant I was. I was mad. My rabbi growing up had lied to me. He misled me. He cheated me and stole my heritage – why didn't he tell me anything? Why did he bore me with his lengthy political dissertations at the High Holiday services? He never gave me a reason to be Jewish. I was listening. I was searching. I was open. Why wasn't he authentic? What was he embarrassed about? What was wrong with being Jewish, looking Jewish, feeling Jewish, or telling the world you are Jewish?

I remembered something I saw my rabbi do when I was in high school. Back then I still worked for my dad. I worked at the same chemical factory I worked at when I was thirteen (except now they paid me better). We went to work early in the morning to beat traffic. We ate breakfast at a diner on the highway along way. Our rabbi ate there too: he ordered eggs, sausage, and toast. He wore his yarmulke and looked very rabbinic. I didn't care at the time.

But now I was incensed. What was he doing there? What kind of rabbi hangs out in a diner eating non-kosher food? He was a sellout. He was phony and I hated him. I hated him with every fiber of my being. He was a fake and his Judaism was a lie: he didn't believe it himself. He stole my heritage, turned me off, and sent me away. He made me wander until I was twenty-five. He made me hate myself. He made me want to be black and jealous of the

Italians. He made me search in music, books, knish shops, and travel to find meaning. I was empty yet the answers I was looking for were right under my nose. They were right there and my bozo rabbi hid them from me with his church organ, shiksa girlfriend (he converted her himself), smoking, liberal politics, and all the garbage he stood for. I saw him for what he was: an arrogant, self-righteous, self-aggrandizing, egotistical fool. Yuck.

I understood why Malcolm X clicked with me: I was as mad as hell. I was just like him, my identity was sold to the lowest bidder and I was left envying a culture that wasn't mine.

I decided to become as Jewish as possible. I grew my beard even longer and embraced every outward exhibition of visible Jewishness I could find. I wore a yarmulke, *tzitzis*, *Tefillin*, picked up Hebrew and Yiddish expressions, and grew wings behind my ears. I was the fully realized, newly identified, suddenly actualized poster child for the Jewish people.

"Dude, have you ever tried Shabbos?" My beard was immense. I was one of those guys with the big wooly yarmulkes, flannel, and a guitar slung on his back. I was weird. "Shabbos man, you have to try Shabbos. You will dig it man. It is so Jewish, so real, so Shabbos." I was out of my mind. I ate health food. I walked barefoot in the sand. I was one with my land and my people and my heritage and everything. I was never going to leave Israel. I was the Earth Jew. I studied all day, ate kosher food, dug Shabbos, argued with everyone, thought about everything, and reinterpreted the world through my Jew-colored glasses. I was insane and crazy and mad with Judaism.

And it was fine. No one complained. I was annoying and it didn't matter. My friends tolerated me and put up with my shenanigans; most guys go through a fit of insanity when they come into contact with an authentic expression of their heritage. I was no exception. My friends understood me – they went through it themselves. I would grow out of it.

But then I had to go home. After six months on the road and another eight months in Israel I had to go home. I knew this before I left. My cousin was getting married in June 1994. He got engaged before I left and it was known that I would be back for the wedding – I was the best man.

But now I was insane. I was a radical Jewish lunatic smack in the middle of my new Jewish growing pains. It was going to take time to grow out of it. But what to do?

I didn't want to go back to Amsterdam to catch my flight home (not that it still existed, I missed the deadline). I convinced my parents that they needed to buy me a new ticket. I told them I needed a round trip ticket or I wasn't coming. They weren't happy about it, but they went along with it, and in June 1994 the Earth Jew was in New York City.

The world would never be the same.

My plane landed in New York. I was home for the first time after 14 months on the road. I was a sight to behold – skinny body, big beard, exotic headgear, suit – I lost a ton of weight traveling (eating nothing and walking around all day does that). I was less than 130 pounds. I seemed serious. My shirt was tucked into my pants (something I never did). I stopped using foul language. My family couldn't figure out what happened.

My parents picked me up at the airport and were prepared for the worst: someone told them I was in a cult. We had an awkward talk on the trip back from the airport. "I believe in God." Weird. Where did that come from? I was jetlagged and exhausted, which didn't help. In Jerusalem I was extreme, but understood and tolerated. In America I was some kind of hippie-medieval-modern-relic thing. Authentic? Trying? Out of place was more like it.

The kitchen was stocked with kosher food. My parents are cool and were going to make the best of it. They left me alone when I prayed in the basement. I couldn't relax. I wasn't the carefree nut they knew or the edgy New Yorker who left a year and a half ago. I was serious and Jewish looking. My family couldn't relate to the Earth Jew or my struggle for identity or my need for meaning or any of that. They couldn't figure out why I was throwing my life away to live in Israel and study all day. But at least I was going to marry a Jewish girl.

I went to my cousin's wedding. My aunt ordered a kosher airline meal for me and it was served sealed in plastic: I wouldn't let them open it in the kitchen and the Styrofoam box was fused onto the plastic wrapping by the Microwave. I tore at the wrapping with a plastic knife and got gravy on the maid of honor's dress. Awkward. It was going to be a long trip.

I assaulted my family with authentic Judaism. I was out of my mind. I kept Shabbos, boiled my pots and pans, bought button-down shirts, over analyzed everything, suffered silently, taught impromptu Torah lessons to my relatives, mourned the intermarriage in my family, shunned TV, and made fanatic and unnecessary stands about kosher food and Shabbos observance. I prayed when I came out of the bathroom and before I ate.

Aside from the wedding I didn't have much to do. My turntable stopped working while I was away and all my best music was on vinyl. I decided to go to New York to see if I could find my friends.

I got in touch with Botz. After I left, Botz landed a gig with Eddie, a blues guitarist who played with John Lee Hooker in the 1950s. Eddie was the real thing. He was old, black, and on the road all year long. Botz toured with him for months on end, playing music almost every night. He got to see all of Continental America and most of the Canadian Provinces too. He wasn't getting rich from the gig, but he got paid regularly and felt like a real musician. He was getting back together with his ex-wife.

It was a fluke that we were both in town at the same time. We met up in the Village and walked around. It was summer and hot. Miniskirts were in. I wanted to tell Botz everything. I wanted to tell him all about what happened to me: what I saw, what I found, what I dug in Israel, about *it*, how the band had *it*, how what we had was only a taste, how there was so much more, Simchas Torah, my conservative tribal roots, the intensity of the music, the land, not being a minority, being authentic and real and deep, meaning, Shabbos and the Earth Jew – I was out of breath with excitement. He was my brother. He taught me how to drive in New York. He understood me. I wanted to bear my soul and dump it on his lap.

Botz wasn't interested. You can't sum up 14 months of experiences, feelings, emotions, and revelations in a conversation. He didn't get it. He spent most of the day looking at legs and counting the number of beautiful women he saw.

Al joined us in the afternoon. The two of them talked about women – New York women, women on the road, summer women versus winter women, dating women – they kept track of all the women on the street that day; rating, tallying, and arguing about bodies. I was in a different world. I went through so much. I found *it*. Botz and Al were not impressed. I was the odd man out, I walked behind them as we wandered the city and they talked and joked about women.

We were starving. I convinced them to get knishes. Al wanted pizza but I prevailed. We went to Delancey Street. We found one of the knish places I used to visit; when I started thinking about being Jewish and the only thing I identified with was food.

We ordered. The owner walked in. He looked at me and told me he wouldn't serve me. "We are only kosher style, not really kosher. Sorry. You're too religious. This place is not for you." Botz and Al ate knishes and I starved. Al felt bad for me and didn't complain about the food.

We spent the rest of the day like this. We walked around. Al and Botz rated women. I starved. We talked about music. "We should go to Brooklyn and jam." Impossible – no drums – Botz was only home for a few days before going back on the road. His gear was in Georgia on the way to the next gig.

I left them and went uptown to hang out with Josh. Josh was still living in his swank apartment on the Upper East Side. He was still painting, crazy, and claiming to be poor and misunderstood. We listened to avant-garde jazz and talked. We talked for three days. We talked until we fell asleep, slept, got up, and talked some more. We started talking in his apartment in New York, went to my parent's house in New Jersey, and kept on talking – all the time listening to pretentious music.

Josh was freaked out, defensive, and unable to deal with me. A year and a half ago we were exactly the same: two Jewish guys living in New York searching for meaning, identity, and digging music and art. I made a radical break and moved on. Josh couldn't do it. He couldn't leave the comfort and excuses of not doing anything. He stayed in

New York and he was never leaving New York. He painted. He wrote pretentious rants without punctuation and in all capital letters. He couldn't have a normal conversation with me. True, we talked for three days, but our conversation was Josh asking questions, not listening to my answers, and asking more questions about something unrelated. He was defensive, argued, and distanced himself from what I was telling him. It didn't help that I was out of my mind, fanatic, unbalanced, insecure, and only had a superficial understanding of what I was doing. We argued and talked. Josh didn't listen. I ranted. The music played. We accomplished nothing.

Music is something we always talked about. We met because Josh loved Zappa and wanted to take guitar lessons. I turned him on to the blues. We listened to Muddy Waters, John Lee Hooker, Howlin' Wolf, Sonny Boy Williamson, and all the classic players when we weren't listening to pretentious art-jazz.

Josh put on a Fuzzy Walter record. It was awesome. I was in the zone. So what if I was the Earth Jew? Nothing beats authentic blues. Fuzzy Walter was the blues equivalent of a Jew living in the Judean Desert, walking the footsteps of the patriarchs.

"Would you tour with Fuzzy Walter?" Josh asked. Of course I would, what kind of stupid question was that? The Fuzzy Walter Band was the most coveted gig in the blues. He was old but still touring and still awesome. "But I thought you were about being authentic? How would you do both?" An innocent question: how could I be the authentic tribal Jew, one with his land and his people, *and* tour with Fuzzy Walter? It was impossible.

He got me. I didn't know how to answer him. I was a walking contradiction. I couldn't have my old life and dreams and also my new life and identity.

I didn't know how to answer him. Josh went home. I bought toiletries and things I wasn't able to find in Israel. I spent my last few days talking to my parents, visiting family, and hanging out in New Jersey.

✧ 10 ✧

I went back to Israel and moved into my room at the yeshiva, but the daily routine of prayer and study was different. Josh had thrown me for a loop. His question raised an issue I didn't want to deal with. I wanted to play music, tour the world, and hang with the blues crowd. But I wanted to be the Earth Jew too, isolated in Israel, the yeshiva, and Jewishness.

I discussed my inner conflict with my friends in Israel. They couldn't relate. "Judaism is real. What are you stressing about? If God exists then He exists, forget this other stuff." It didn't help. I needed an answer.

Summer ended and the winter semester started. I took classes during the day and was expected to study at night. I spent most of my time at the yeshiva.

The yeshiva's building was old and typical of the Old City buildings rebuilt after the Six Day War. Our building was a hodgepodge of four apartments knocked into one. The original apartments were on a hill and at different levels and heights. Odd stairways and awkward arches connected the converted apartments to each other. The main library was a large room in the center of the complex. Off the library at one end were two small classrooms. At the other end were two rooms connected to an exterior hallway. Bookshelves lined every wall and makeshift shelves were set up over windows. The books were beat, like the building itself, but the place had a warmth and old school charm.

No one used the classrooms at night. I hid in one every night after dinner and blocked the door so nobody could get in. I paced back and forth. My mind wandered. I thought about my travels, the band, the books I read, the yeshiva, Judaism, and my trip home. I tried to make sense of it.

I thought about Josh and our awkward, endless conversation in New York. "Would you take the gig?" "Of course I would take the gig." "How could you?" How could I? How could I not?

The question was in my head on an infinite repeat. I wanted the gig. But I wanted to be in Israel. I wanted *it*. Fuzzy Walter had *it*. I could have *it* touring in his band. But I had *it* in Israel. If I could get *it* touring with Fuzzy Walter, I didn't need Israel and all the Jewish stuff. In Israel I was authentic; I was primal, tribal, and real. Authentic is cool. But if *it* was what I really wanted, I could have it without Israel. I didn't *have* to be authentic. Why torture my family? Why be weird?

"Would you take the gig?" My brain was like a broken record. "Yes I would take the gig." "What are you doing in Israel?" "Shut up. You are driving me crazy."

It went on like this for a few weeks. I was agitated. It wouldn't go away. Until finally I had a breakthrough: I decided that Josh's question was irrelevant. Touring with Fuzzy Walter wasn't the issue. The issue was something else.

"Would you want Fuzzy Walter to be your father?"

Would I want him to be my father? No. Why not? It was a good question. Fuzzy Walter was the boogieman, the greatest blues musician alive, but he would be a lousy father. He was never around. He took a lot of drugs. He was a womanizer. His life offstage was a disaster.

When Fuzzy Walter was on stage he gave you *it*. He took you to a place you couldn't get to on your own and held you there. You never wanted it to end. You wanted it to last forever. You were knee deep in *it*.

But it always ended. You always went home – and so did Fuzzy Walter. And he went home to a mess. Yes, he was a great musician, but otherwise he was a loser. And there is more to life than being a great musician.

Great music is only a tiny piece of the puzzle. What about the rest of my life? What about the hours and hours when I wasn't playing music, when I was bored and alone, what about them? Something made me leave New York. There was a reason I related to Henry Miller and was inspired to travel and see Paris.

Fuzzy Walter took drugs and tried to forget about it. I wanted to figure it out. I knew that life had more to offer than a temporary high, even if the high was intense.

I wasn't thinking when I left New York. I just did it because I was missing something. If I stayed in New York I would have been just like Josh, a big, fat, dumb, idiot wallowing in self-pity and making excuses. Call it angst.

Forget angst. Give me gestalt.

Something clicked when I got to Israel and it was about more than being surrounded by Jews and the emotional trip of discovering my identity. It was bigger than that.

I discovered that the high I was searching for was something I had all along; I just needed to access it. Music is a part of it – the experience is real – but so is eating a sandwich, making a commitment, laughing, failing a test, talking to a friend, sitting in traffic, and getting angry at the bank.

I wanted the secret of *it*. I wanted the meaning of life. I discovered that it isn't a secret and it isn't that deep. I had to internalize this lesson before I could tour with Fuzzy Walter.

The meaning of life is to love being alive. I wanted to do it all the time.

Part Two

The Shema was the first religious thing I tried.[1] The Shema was cool. I liked the way it felt in my mouth. I dug the sound of the letters and the mantra like quality of it, and it was hip to say words in an exotic, ancient language.

Someone helped me transliterate the Shema into English characters so I could say it in Hebrew. Saying it in English wasn't cool: English was antithetical to the tribal, new, primal culture I was getting into. I wrote it out on a few pages of Israeli notebook paper and carried it around everywhere. I got used to saying it. I said it every day. I dug the sounds. I sometimes said the whole thing and sometimes just worked through the first sentence. I made it into a rhythm and goofed with the words in odd time signatures. I thought about using it is a part of a fugue, similar to what Bach did with Christian liturgy. I pronounced the words every day, but I didn't know what they meant.

I did this for a few months. I kept the handwritten transliteration folded in my pocket and it got worn from use. After a while, the novelty of reading something in an ancient language wore off, but I kept doing it and got into the habit of saying it every morning. I eventually bought a Hebrew/English prayer book, read the translation every day in addition to the transliteration, and learned the meaning of the Shema.

Learning the meaning of the Shema was my entrance into the world of Jewish philosophy. I didn't know it at the time, but the Shema is the national anthem, apple pie, mom, and football of Judaism: the fundamentals. Jewish law mandates that it should be said every morning and evening. It is one of the first things you teach your kids and it is supposed to be the last thing you say before you die. It is written on parchment and affixed to the doors of every room in your house. Jewish men wrap it to their bodies every morning in black leather boxes.

The first sentence is the mother load; it provides a working definition of God. You can't discuss spirituality, morality, ethics, religion, philosophy – or anything for that matter – without definitions. And you can't discuss Judaism without defining God.

The Shema defines God as the unlimited source of existence.[2] God is not energy, a thing, Santa Claus, a sweet old man with a checklist, the goodness within you, or George Burns smoking a cigar in your shower. God doesn't sit on a cloud in the sky taking notes to see if you earned enough points to get into heaven. God is the unlimited source of existence. He has all the power. He is the master of reality. Everything that happens is a manifestation of what He wants. In simple language – God is the source of reality. Or more simply – God *is* reality.[3]

I was frustrated back when I lived in Brooklyn because I only knew a pop-culture definition of God: i.e. some sort of mythical-tooth-fairy-energy-thing. Based on that definition, I decided there was nothing, when you died you were dead, and that apathy was an art. But I was dishonest. Deep down I believed in God. When I was mad I yelled at God. When I was sad I complained to God. When I needed something I prayed to God. I believed in something. I just didn't call it God. The Jewish definition – God as reality – was a practical definition I could live with.

I needed practical. A girl I knew in New York told me about her friend who read the Kabbalah. I didn't know what the Kabbalah was. She said it was Jewish mysticism. That was cool. I never heard of Jewish mysticism. Her friend went crazy after he finished reading it. Very impractical: Jewish mysticism made you crazy. I didn't look into it. I didn't have the patience. I didn't look into Taoism, transcendental meditation, or taking peyote with Indian medicine men either.

The next idea in the Shema – after defining God – is "loving God." The first time I heard about "loving God" it made me uncomfortable. Bible-thumping, fundamentalist Christians talk about loving God. I thought they were nuts. "Loving God" is an archaic, religious, esoteric concept I didn't relate to.

But if you define God as reality, loving God is an easy concept to digest. Loving God means loving reality. It isn't a dumb Christian thing. It is a practical concept that makes sense. It works. I can love reality.

And this broke a massive misconception I had about Jews and religion. I thought Judaism was a boring thing you did twice a year (plus Chanukah, presents, Passover, and grandma singing *Dayainu* really loud). Religious Jews were ultra-fanatic Hasidim: they lived in a bubble, had sex through a sheet, owned most of Brooklyn, only ate kosher food, prayed all day, had fifteen kids, and were usually miserable. I didn't know any better. Religious Jews might as well have been Martians. I didn't know the Shema was about life. Nobody told me.

I wanted to love life. I was frustrated because the best moments happened by accident – the band, driving with Botz, Italian food, the boat ride with Kofi, Prague – these were random, lucky, unexpected, unplanned experiences. They were incredible and then it was over. The experience was fleeting. If God is reality – and your job is to love reality – then there must be a way to love everything: like the line at the bank, a sandwich, airport security, a nice day, friends, cooking onions, bugs, extra virgin olive oil, traffic, and everything else. You don't need luck if you know what you are doing. A great conversation can be as awesome as seeing AC/DC in a small club or meeting Jack Kerouac on a street corner in Denver. You need a system, tools, discipline, patience, and effort to live with this level of focus, but at least Judaism is dedicated to reality.

Love reality: that is the secret of Jewish spirituality.[4] Praying, fasting, meditating, incense, organic food, candles, Patchouli oil, rice paper, and bamboo rugs are not the only pathways to spirituality. You don't need to do something *spiritual* to connect to reality.

Think about it.

If doing something spiritual was the only way to have a spiritual experience, then spirituality would be no different than touring with Fuzzy Walter, listening to music, reading a book, traveling, digging great art, or anything else. Spirituality would just be another temporary high. Your connection to reality would be fleeting. It would end when the meditation ended, the prayer finished, or when the incense burned out. Real spirituality must include physicality too.[5] The system should be holistic.

The first great Jewish writer I read was Maimonides. He wrote a massive, fourteen-volume code of Jewish Law.

The fifth volume is called *The Book of Holiness*. *The Book of Holiness* could be about anything. Most people assume it is about praying, holidays, souls, fasting, God, meditating, or any other thing you consider holy. But it isn't. *The Book of Holiness* only deals with two topics. On the surface these two topics are antithetical to what you think is holy.

The Book of Holiness is about food and sex.[6]

Shocking. I thought religious people thought food and sex were dirty. Holy people were monks, hermits, celibate, and weird. They lived in caves, organic farms, mountaintops, communes, and mud huts. Holy people didn't understand real life. They drank molasses, ate flaxseed, fasted three or four days a week, and slept in odd cycles – usually after eighteen-hour meditations or extreme tests of self-endurance. They didn't bathe, talk, cut their hair, or have anything to do with mundane things like food and sex.

But the Jewish path to holiness is different. The holiest people have tons of kids. You eat more on holy days. You need a job, relationships, money, a house, and interaction with other people. Even prayer – a private and intense experience – is done as part of a community.

Food and sex are spiritual paths. That makes sense. If God exists – and He really created man – He created man as is. Man has drives and desires: he longs for food, sex, and everything else. Did God create these drives as a joke? Is He sitting in a big chair laughing at people as they stumble over themselves? "Look at how holy that person is. HAHA. Holy. Watch him pray. Now watch him check out the woman in the next pew! HAHA." What kind of sadistic god would that be? Obviously you can get out of hand, too much food and sex are destructive.[7] You need to learn how to harness these drives. But when you understand that these desires are spiritual tools – wow – you can experience the ultimate all the time.

Spirituality is normal. The battle is staying focused.

It takes effort to stay focused. Talking about lofty ideas isn't enough. I rambled for two days on the boat with Kofi. The conversation was intense. But that was about it. We never decided to do anything. I followed him to Jerusalem to crash on a floor and bum around for a few more weeks.

You need to make an effort. Without focus you aren't alive. You exist.[8] You need more than a punch-the-clock, nine-to-five, lumber-through-life existence. Your soul longs for it.

When I worked for the Philharmonic I took the subway every morning. I saw the same people everyday. They were miserable. The men wore suits and red power ties. The women wore skits, commuter sneakers, and socks they changed when they got to the office. Everyone wore headphones. The subway seats were an endless row of faces and headphones: people turned off to the world. No one spoke or made eye contact. "Turn up the volume and don't think." These people were the same every day. Yesterday they were miserable. Tomorrow they will still be miserable. The headphones were a distraction. It stopped them from thinking about how miserable they were.

But staying focused is only half the battle. Constant spirituality requires a change in perspective. You need to know that everything – everything you own and every experience – is an opportunity.[9] The trick is taking advantage of every opportunity.

Warren Zevon said it best. He went on the David Letterman Show a few weeks before he died. He had inoperable lung cancer and everyone knew he was dying. Letterman asked him, "Is there anything you know now that you want to tell others?" Zevon replied, "Savor every sandwich."

Don't miss out. Life is awesome. It is a Jewish idea to know that life is awesome. Make the effort, stay focused, and learn the rules to get the most out of life.

Life comes with instructions. Everything does.

You can't play the guitar, drive a car, boil pasta, balance your checkbook, pass an exam, lift weights, change your oil, or send an email without instructions. You have to learn what to do.

Everything is like this. You need to learn tools, methods, rules, systems, and techniques. Without them you are lost. You can wing it – and for little things it doesn't matter – but you wouldn't want your doctor to wing it (or your mechanic, accountant, or bus driver). You expect them to know what they are doing. You need instructions for life too.

The Torah is the Jewish instruction manual. The word "Torah" means "instructions." The Torah is a set of instructions for life (*Toras Chaim*). [10] The idea is that if you follow the instructions, you will get the most out of life.

Radical. It never occurred to me that life came with instructions (and certainly not Jewish instructions). It was too much. My entire adventure was about the *process*, finding *it*. I didn't think about the next step: *doing* it.

The Jewish system, the Torah, is a complete system. It is loaded with tools to get the most out of life. Food, sex, money, speech, work, community, meditation, family, death, birth, emotions, education – the Torah discusses everything.[11] But it isn't easy. Putting the system into practice takes discipline and patience. There are bumps and growing pains along the way. In my case, I got weird, argued with people, studied all day, and became the Earth Jew. Other people run away.

There is a fear factor too. The Torah is overwhelming. It has a lot of rules. The rules are daunting and they seem to have strings attached. You have to pray all day. You can't rip toilet paper on Shabbos. You can't eat anything. Terrifying. I had visions of men shaking back and forth, unable to have a normal conversation in English, wearing black hats and black clothes.

But this fear of Torah – like most fear – is the fear of the unknown. Judaism is a discipline like anything else. The rules don't make sense out of context. It takes years of practice and study to become an expert.

Think about it.

When you first learned how to read, did you just open a book and read? No. Someone showed you a bunch of lines and shapes and told you that these were "letters." Each letter represented a specific sound. Some letters made more than one sound. Combinations of letters made different sounds: T+H is "th" and G+H is "f." It didn't make sense. But you studied, learned more sounds and rules, and practiced. You slowly put sounds together, made words, and eventually understood what you were reading. As an adult, reading is second nature. You don't think about what you're doing.

Every discipline is like this – whether it is meditating, cooking, driving, swimming, accounting, riding a bike, computer programming, or anything – the process is always the same. You learn a set of rules. A lot of it seems weird. Sometimes the system is huge and overwhelming. You have to practice and make an effort. But eventually you can do it. If you become an expert, doing it seems natural, almost second nature.

Once you master a system, the rules give you freedom. They enable you to express yourself.

I play the guitar. I started taking guitar lessons when I was thirteen. I went to my first lesson and my teacher gave me a ton of rules. He told me, "Keep your thumb in the middle of the neck. Arch your fingers. Keep your palm off the neck. Pick up and down." He didn't explain advanced concepts in music theory or how Jimi Hendrix got his tone on *Voodoo Child*. He showed me basic rules so I could make a sound on the instrument. I practiced and did everything he showed me. I didn't sound very good.

He gave me more rules at my next lesson, "This is how you make a bar. Make sure to limit your hand motion. These are different chord shapes and scales." The list was endless. By the end of my first year I knew at least a hundred rules.

I persevered. I practiced. By the end of high school I was the most boring guitarist in the world. I knew a lot of rules but I couldn't do anything. I kept practicing.

I started playing professionally in college. Something happened. On stage with my band, during solos, I created colors and textures. I didn't think, "I have to hold the guitar like this and use this shape to produce this sound." I just did it. I moved my hands and the color came out. I had internalized the rules and the system. What was once a restrictive discipline was now a vehicle for self-expression.

The Torah is a system for spiritual self-expression. It is hard work. The rules are difficult. It takes practice and effort. But if you make the effort, you master the skills to love reality and experience the pleasure of being alive. It takes a book as big as the Talmud[12] to explain how the Jewish system is applied in every area. It is certainly beyond the scope of this book.

But I found what I was looking for. It took twenty-five years – I had to travel halfway around the world to find it – but it was worth it. Life is awesome; you just need to make an effort and know what you are doing.

The joke is that it was right under my nose the whole time.

Outro

I asked my wife to read the first-draft of this book. She is an honest critic and a good judge of my writing. I thought I came off as a slick, early-nineties hipster, looking for meaning and adventure.

My wife didn't agree. "This is funny." She said. "You were a typical Jewish kid from New Jersey and a real mama's boy. You know the type? You wanted to be cool and fit in. But you were a nerd and socially awkward. You didn't take drugs. You didn't do anything bad. But you tried. Cute. But sad. I can't believe I married a dweeb."

Oh well.

This book told my story. I thought I was cool. My wife says I was a dork. It doesn't matter. I was looking for something. I traveled. I read. I ate knishes. I thought I was the Jewish Malcolm X.

And I encountered a lot of people who were looking for something too.

Think about it. I connected with a lot of people. I had a lot of intense conversations. I read books that sold a lot of copies. The places I visited were Bohemian Meccas. I wasn't unique. The things I tried were standard. But it was an adventure nonetheless. Searching for answers is something you have to do. The rub – at least for me – was that the answers were somehow Jewish. It never occurred to me that Judaism had anything to offer. Nobody told me. It blew my mind.

I wrote this book to tell my story. I thought it was a good way to teach a Jewish lesson, namely that it is a Jewish idea to live an incredible life. I think the book does this – but my story is really about something else.

When I was twenty-five I decided to do something. I was sick of New York. I was missing something. I was lost. I didn't have an identity.

So I decided to leave. I didn't know what I was doing. I didn't know if it would work out. I didn't think about it or make a plan. I just did it. Did I do the right thing? I don't know. But I stopped complaining and got on with my life.

This book is about doing something. The most important day in my life was my first day in Amsterdam – I was timid, I needed to grow up – but I learned something profound. I was confused when I lived in Brooklyn. I philosophized but I didn't know what I was talking about. The sign on my wall said, "apathy is an art." It was wrong. Apathy isn't an art. Apathy is your enemy.

Appendix

Shwarma: A Love Story

Many of my musician friends took a lot of drugs. They were trying to recreate the high of performing during the times when they weren't performing. I looked into meditation. I dug the eastern flavor.

But meditation was hard. I couldn't do it. Too many years of drinking coffee made it impossible to sit still for more than five minutes. I bounced off the walls. My eyes flickered. My nose twitched. But I wasn't willing to accept my spiritual impotence. I blamed the world around me.

"I hate hippies," I told a friend.

"Why? What did they do to you?"

"They ruin my inner peace and they smell. I hate the smell of Patchouli oil."

I knew meditation wasn't for me, but I stuck with it. I read books about Taoist philosophy, *Naked Lunch*, music and religion, and a few other books about spirituality. At some point I started thinking about being Jewish. I bought a book about Jewish meditation. I bought the book to justify my growing interest in Judaism but still look cool in the eyes of the art crowd.

I tried to do what the book suggested. I gazed at letters in the Hebrew alphabet. I thought about various interpolations of the different names of God. I drove myself crazy.

I discussed Jewish meditation with a friend. "I can't find the space behind my head!" "What are you talking about?" He said. "The book says, 'focus on the space behind your head.'" I said. "I keep thinking about dandruff and male pattern baldness. This isn't spirituality. It's insanity."

I persevered. "Maybe God's a practical joker," I said.

"Why?"

"The vehicles to transcendence are totally unnatural. Who can sit around all day clearing his brain of static?"

"Maybe you're looking in the wrong place."

"Maybe. I'm always hungry."

A Middle Eastern friend turned me on to my first shwarma.

"Come. I give you experience," he said.

"Great."

He took me to a greasy Israeli joint. We sat down. The guy behind the counter brought out what looked like an overweight tortilla.

"Lafa," my friend informed me.

"What's that?"

"It like giant flat pita. You no stuff it. You roll it."

The guy behind the counter slapped on a thick helping of crushed chickpea paste.

"Humus," my friend said.

"I know."

The guy behind the counter loaded it up with chopped cucumber salad, French fries and a mysterious meat substance.

"Lamb," my friend said.

"Lamb?"

"Really turkey. But basted all day in lamb fat. Delicious."

The guy behind the counter rolled it up and handed it to me. I took a bite. Grease ran down my arm.

"This is unbelievable," I said.

"I knew you like it."

The feeling stayed with me for almost a week. It was in my head. It was on my breath. I knew I was on to something big. I extolled the virtues of shwarma to everyone. It was all I talked about.

"What! You haven't had shwarma? You haven't lived," I told people.

I ran into some of my meditating friends. "How can you spend your day sitting around like a lotus? There is shwarma to be eaten." "We're into connecting to a higher reality," they said. "So am I. It's called shwarma."

I found it. I thought I had to do something *spiritual* to experience spirituality. I was wrong. True transcendence isn't about slipping into an artificial world. It is about finding spirituality in the here and now. Shwarma isn't a meal. It is a connection to reality.

I taught people about higher eating. I explained that there are two ways to eat shwarma:

Inhale – open wide and swallow – similar to the way a dog eats – *or* –

Pause before eating and say, "Isn't it great that I can live in a world where I can have an experience like shwarma?" And then inhale.

The first way is to eat the shwarma because it is shwarma. The second way is to use the shwarma as a spiritual vehicle: realize that this meal is an opportunity to connect to God, i.e. focus, plug in, and experience transcendence.

I discovered that shwarma contained the secret to higher living: elevate the physical. Life is a tool to connect to something bigger.

Sometimes a person needs to take time out to think about things, to meditate. Most of the time he just needs to eat something greasy.

Groovy Photos

Senior Prom. I am wearing an official Don Johnson Miami Vice tuxedo. It is mauve and came with a free pair of Ray-Ban sunglasses. If you look closely, you will notice the beginnings of a mullet just below my ears.

Fat Elvis on stage at Boston's Jordan Hall. On the right is Gerald, our drummer. In the middle is Dean, our bass player. I am on the left. Dig the hair and Fu Manchu moustache.

Cut my hair but still cool. I am in our rehearsal space in Brooklyn.

Publicity Photo 1990.

The Mellow Edwards outside CBGB's in Manhattan. The Mellow Edwards played free jazz/heavy metal and featured lead trombone and rhythm guitar. We were one of the first bands to play at CB's Gallery, an art space run by CBGB's. This was my last gig before I left for Europe.

At Jim Morrison's grave in Paris.

Oh so cool. Self-portrait in a bathroom in Prague.

98 ✧ *Everything You Want Is Really Jewish*

Transitioning.

The Earth Jew fully realized. I am standing with Shimon, my roommate from Manipur, India. He is now a rabbi and lives in Kiryat Arba (when he isn't in Afghanistan, making Shabbos for the Mujahideen).

Endnotes

[1] The Shema is a standard part of the daily liturgy. It is comprised of three paragraphs taken from different parts of the Torah. Deuteronomy 6:4-9. Deuteronomy 11:13-21. Numbers 15:37-41.

[2] See Shulchan Aruch O.C. 5. "When a person mentions the name of God, he should a) concentrate on the explanation of the name he says (Adono-y): understand that He is 'Master of All Reality.' And b) he should concentrate on the written form of the name and understand that He 'is, was, and always will be.' When he mentions the 'Elokim' name he should intend that He is 'All-Able and All-Powerful.'" The Mishna Berurah quotes the Vilna Goan (M.B. 5:3) and explains further, "[A person] doesn't need to have this focus every time he mentions the name of God, except when reading the Shema…"

The point here is that when you say the Shema you have to think that God is: a) Master of all reality, b) is, was, and always will be, and c) all-powerful. The first verse of Shema concludes, "God is one." In other words, He is the only reality, the only reality not bound by time, and the only power – or more simply – the unlimited source of existence.

[3] Technically speaking, you can't define God as *anything*. Rabbi Moshe Chaim Luzzatto makes this point over and over again in

the *Da'as T'vunos*. As my teacher, Rabbi Yochanan Bechhofer explained Rabbi Luzzatto, "You can't know what God is. You can only know what God does. And really you can't even know that – you can only know the *results* of what He did." Based on this understanding it is only correct (at most) to call God "the source of reality." However, for the sake of simplicity – and particularly since this is how man relates to Him – I chose here to refer to God as "reality." My Rosh Yeshiva, Rabbi Noah Weinberg ztz'l, often referred to God simply as "reality" as well.

[4] See the *Path of the Just* by Rabbi Moshe Chaim Luzzatto, "Our sages of blessed memory have taught us that man was created for the sole purpose of rejoicing in God and deriving pleasure from the splendor of His Presence; for this is the true joy and the greatest pleasure that can be found." He goes on to explain, "The place where this joy may truly be derived is the World to Come, which was expressly created to provide for it; but the path to the object of our desires is this world, as our Sages of blessed memory have said (Avos 4:21), 'This world is like a corridor to the World to Come.'" (Translated by Shraga Silverstein. Published by Feldheim Publishers, 1987.)

You might ask, "Isn't the pleasure in the Next World, not this one?" I think the answer is as Rabbi Luzzatto explains in the *Da'as T'vunos*, "The Highest Will wanted that man should complete himself and that everything was created for this purpose. This itself is man's privilege and reward. Privilege: because man finds that he labors and makes the effort to achieve this completion – and when he achieves it – he will get pleasure only from the effort he made and his portion from all his efforts. Reward: because in the end he is complete."

In other words, the process itself is pleasurable.

See also, Maimonides in the Laws of Repentance, chapter 9.

[5] See the Babylonian Talmud, Berachos, page 54A: "With all your heart (Deuteronomy 6:5), with your two inclinations – your inclination for good and your inclination for bad." The Talmud is explaining why the Torah uses an alternative spelling for the

Hebrew word for heart. The word is usually spelled "L B" but here it is spelled "L B B." The Talmud's explanation is that the extra letter is coming to indicate that man should serve God with *both* his hearts (or *both* his inclinations), i.e. his desire for spirituality as well as his desire for physicality.

⁶ The Book of Holiness is divided into three parts – the Laws of Forbidden Relationships, the Laws of Forbidden Foods, and the Laws of Ritual Slaughter – it discusses a total of seventy commandments and all their details.

⁷ See the Babylonian Talmud, Berachos, page 54A: "With all your soul (Deuteronomy 6:5), even if it takes your soul." The Talmud does not mean that a person should martyr himself for the Jewish people (see Maimonides, the Laws of the Foundation of Torah, chapter 5 for a discussion about Jewish martyrdom). It means that a person should focus all his energy on loving God. A person who fails to love God is not called alive. He merely exists.

⁸ See the Babylonian Talmud, Berachos, page 54A: "With all your might (Deuteronomy 6:5), a) with all your money or b) with every measure He metes out to you, be *modeh* to Him (i.e. admit that it comes from Him)." Although most prayer books translate this phrase as "with all your might," it is clear from the Talmud that it is more correct to translate this phrase as either "all your money" or "all your life experiences." In other words, everything you have and everything that happens to you is an opportunity to love God.

⁹ My Rosh Yeshiva, Rabbi Noah Weinberg ztz'l, said this idea all the time. The source is from a class he taught called "The ABC's of Judaism." Defining the Torah as "Instructions for Living" is letter E.

¹⁰ Look over an index for the *Mishna Torah* by Maimonides or *The Code of Jewish Law* by Rabbi Joseph Caro – you will quickly conclude that Judaism discusses everything.

¹¹ The standard edition of the Talmud published today is a twenty-volume set. In many Jewish communities, one page of Talmud is studied every day (a "page" is both sides of a page, front and back). It takes about seven and a half years to complete the entire cycle.

Acknowledgements

So many wonderful people helped make this book possible. To all the people in my life who turned up in these stories (and those who didn't), you gave so much to me and I never properly thanked you – forgive me and accept my warmest and most sincere appreciation for all the support, patience, and tolerance you showed me.

I changed all the names of the people who appear in this book. I left the names of the famous people I referenced as is, unless they interacted with me personally (like, who is Taylor McKnight and Fuzzy Walter anyway?).

Thank you to Esther Zaretsky for her wonderful job editing, typesetting, designing the cover, and layout. She put in countless hours and her selflessness and dedication know no bounds. A big thank you is also in store for Alina Koyfman for her proofreading and editing (particularly discovering typos, inconsistencies, and bad grammar). Thank you to Shmuel and D'vora Miller for your friendship, moral support, and initial proofreading as well.

I owe a big thank you and a debt of gratitude to my good friend Alexander Seinfeld – he helped me navigate the crazy world of books, ISBN, and bar codes. His assistance was essential in making this project possible.

I can never repay the debt of gratitude I owe my rabbi and teacher Rabbi Noah Weinberg ztz'l. He was a role model to so many and a great leader of the Jewish people, but to me he was a constant source of encouragement, support, clarity, and guidance. His focus, determination, vision, and inspiration will be sorely missed.

A big thank you is also in store for the entire staff of Aish HaTorah, particularly those who helped me, fostered my growth, and tolerated my insanity over the years. Thank you to Rabbi Eric Coopersmith, Rabbi Nechemia Coopersmith, Rabbi Raphael Shore, Rabbi Avraham Manolson, and Rabbi Hillel Weinberg for their support of this project and for providing such a beautiful endorsement.

A special thank you to Rabbi Naftoli Bier, Rosh Kollel of the Kollel of Greater Boston, for his kind words and beautiful approbation for this book. Finding the Kollel was the most important thing that happened to me upon moving to Boston. It is my second home and my only anchor to Torah Judaism. Rabbi Bier, Rabbi Zalman Leff, and their talented staff of rabbis are an unlimited source of wisdom, insight, and kedusha (and also new and interesting expressions in Yiddish). I am privileged and honored that I have the zechus to learn from such holy people.

A massive thank you is in store to all my friends who bought dedications and helped launch this project, and in particular to Chananel Weiner who was instrumental in making the fundraising possible.

This book is dedicated to the loving memory of my father-in-law, Mr. Ian Hyams, on the occasion of his first yahrzeit. He was a special and lovely man, a committed family man, a role model and inspiration to our family, and we love him and miss him dearly. This book is in the zechus of an aliyah for his neshama. A special thanks is in store for my mother-in-law, Mrs. Stephanie Hyams. We love you mum and hope you get particular nachus from this book.

I also have to give a massive thank you to my parents. They were with me from the beginning (obviously), put up with my craziness, tolerated my insanity, gave me the freedom to grow and explore, and as a result I was able to grow up to be a happy and (sort of) normal adult. I love you and wish you much nachus from us and all your grandchildren.

I hope my children aren't shocked by the crazy things their father did and I thank you for letting me get on with this and putting up with all those times I am away. Or worse, when I am home, jet lagged, and not acting like a very good father.

To my dear wife Ruth: you are a source of inspiration and support and I thank you for all you have done and continue to give to me.

More Acknowledgments for the second edition

Thank you again Esther Zaretsky for your invaluable help typesetting the new edition and Shira Greenberg for the amazing new cover.

About the Author

Tzvi Gluckin has been everywhere and done everything. His eclectic tastes and unusual life experiences render him uniquely qualified to discuss a wide array of issues and topics from a fresh and different perspective. His style is unconventional and humorous, his message is powerful and focused, and the experience is inspiring and transformative.

Tzvi Gluckin lectures extensively to English speaking audiences internationally on a wide range of topics. He has served in the Israeli Army, holds a B.M. in Jazz Studies from the New England Conservatory of Music, and received his rabbinical ordination from Rabbi Noah Weinberg *ztz'l* at Aish HaTorah in Jerusalem. Tzvi is the author of four great books including *Knee Deep in the Funk: Under-*

standing the Connection Between Spirituality and Music and the wildly popular *Discover This*. He also recorded *Jewish Roots Music*, a CD of original music. He currently lives in Boston with his wife and children.

Tzvi also loves blogging; visit his blog at www.moretorah.com (and leave comments, it is good for his self esteem).

Rabbinical Endorsements

Erev Pesach 5969

It gives me great pleasure to write an approbation for Tzvi Gluckin's new book, *Everything You Want Is Really Jewish.*

Tzvi first came to Aish HaTorah in 1993. He studied in our Beis Medrash and received his rabbinical ordination from our beloved Rosh Yeshiva, Rabbi Noah Weinberg *ztz'l*.

Tzvi is a talented writer and educator and his skills have been utilized in almost every major program Aish has undertaken since his arrival, including, the Discovery Seminar, Aish Café, the Jerusalem Fellowships, aish.com, Jewel, Essentials, as a teacher in our Beis Medrash, and the list goes on. Tzvi left Jerusalem in 2001 to launch our campus initiative in Boston. He has established himself as a leader in North American outreach and has innovated a number of programs, many of which are now considered standard.

I wish Tzvi much *hatzlocha* in his continued efforts on behalf of *Am Yisroel*.

HaRav Hillel Weinberg
Rosh HaYeshiva

כולל זכרון שרגא פייזל

Boston Academy of Talmudic Research
Founded in memory of Rabbi Philip Cohen
Kollel of Greater Boston, 74 Corey Road, Brighton, MA 02135 (617) 731-8107 FAX (617) 566-7301

Rabbi Naftoly Bier
Rosh Kollel - Dean

Rabbi Zalman Y. Leff
Rosh Kollel - Dean

March 21, 2009

Tzvi Gluckin is a great asset to the Jewish people. The warmth, concern, understanding, patience and tolerance he uniquely conveys with humility and magnanimity to every Jew is invigorating and inspiring.

This coupled with his intellectual gifts and humorous personality is the making of a wonderful teacher, friend, mentor and yes, student.

The average American Jew, entering the new world of university, adulthood and choice of life experience will be at once humored, uplifted, challenged, edified and even see one's mirror-image by the quintessential mind-boggling journey of Tzvi. After reading this book you will have two paths, apathy or resoluteness. It's your choice!

Tzvi: With admiration, I thank you for your sharing your personal global and inner journey with all.

It is my prayer that this book becomes a great asset to those who read it.

With best wishes,

Rabbi Naftoly Bier

Nellie Mael Tape Lending Library · Ezra Polen Judaica Lending Library

Dedications

Ian Marcus Hyams

I met Ian in 1958 when I was 17 years old and knew he was the man I wanted to spend the rest of my life with and we married in 1960.

He was a radio journalist and managed to get many news stories where others had failed, mainly due to his 'chutzpah'. We were living in Nashua New Hampshire when 9/11 happened and as the only BBC reporter available he did 200 broadcasts to the UK in 7 days from a New Jersey hotel and at ground zero, via his cell phone.

He was just 5 feet 2 inches in height, but in personality, warmth & love he was 10 feet tall. There are not enough adjectives to describe him, but suffice to say he was the most loving husband & father to our four children & a wonderful granddad to our nine grandchildren.

His sense of humour was legendary, with Laurel & Hardy being one of his favourite comedy acts and even though he saw them hundreds of times he still exploded with laughter each viewing. In fact I had the logo of their bowler hats etched into each corner of his headstone. He died in April 2008, 3 months after being diagnosed with leukemia and just two months short of our 48th wedding anniversary. I still miss him and not a day goes by without me thinking of him.

Stephanie

I extend my most sincere and heartfelt thanks to the people who contributed to publish the first edition of this book. Looking over this list, I notice that many of you have since gotten married or had children (or both). Isn't life wonderful? I wish you only the very best.

Mrs. Stephanie Hyams
Mr. and Mrs. Robert and Joan Gluckin
Sammy and Reyna Simnegar
Austin Bach
Yitzchok and Marissa Finch
Allan and Sara Sternberg
Adam Sheps
Joseph and Arielle Jaspan
Mazal Mosheyeva
Dmitry Shargorodsky

Discover This
Who Wrote the Torah and How Do You Know?

Can an intelligent, rational, levelheaded, thinking person believe that God wrote the Torah? Good question. *Discover This* is a good answer.

Discover This examines the evidence. Specifically it discusses:

- א   The Contradictory Nature of Jewish Survival
- א   The Jewish Experience at Mount Sinai
- א   The Accuracy of the Torah's Transmission
- א   The Story of the Torah Codes
- א   The Nazis Hidden in the Book of Esther

And much more

Discover This is unleashed, full-throttle, unadulterated, and no-nonsense. It is authoritative, documented, and well researched. It is quality. And it is what you expect, fun to read and easy to understand.

Discover This: Read it. Think about it. And decide for yourself.

Get your copy today: www.gluckin.com/book

Knee Deep in the Funk:
Understanding the Connection Between Spirituality and Music

Music is spiritual - find out how. Learn about the power of the intuitive experience in music; the link between music, sex, drugs, and spirituality; the role of music in meditation and prayer; music as a universal language; and so much more.

Get your copy today: www.gluckin.com/book

*Order more copies of
Everything You Want Is
Really Jewish today!*

*Single orders and bulk rate discounts
are available. Inquire today.*

*For more information and
to book online
visit www.gluckin.com or
email Tzvi directly
at tzvi.gluckin@gmail.com.*

If you liked the book,
you will love the talk!

Bring *Everything You Really Want Is Jewish*
to your community today.

Tzvi Gluckin is an engaging, dynamic, hysterical, thought provoking, and veteran speaker. He is available for every type of speaking engagement including weekend retreats, Shabbatons, full-day seminars, evening programs, high school events, campus programs, young professional events, singles events, keynote addresses, fundraising events, parlor meetings, training sessions, consulting, and every other event, program, seminar, or thing you can think of!

Tzvi has a full array of programs, talks, seminars, and inspirational speeches to chose from. His prices are affordable, negotiable, include perks, and are geared to fit your budget. Tzvi will go the extra mile to make sure you get an amazing program at a price you can afford.

"With his charming personality and disarming sense of humor, Tzvi is able to convey the deepest and most thought provoking of ideas to any audience."
— Rabbi Shimon Kay, Meor Philadelphia

Contact Tzvi today and
bring him to your town!

For more information and to book online
visit www.gluckin.com or email Tzvi
directly at tzvi.gluckin@gmail.com.

www.ingramcontent.com/pod-product-compliance
Lightning Source LLC
Chambersburg PA
CBHW032137040426
42449CB00005B/278